W9-AWB-155

# RENEWING CATECHETICAL MINISTRY

# RENEWING CATECHETICAL MINISTRY

## A Future Agenda

RICHARD REICHERT

PAULIST PRESS
New York/Mahwah, N.J.

Excerpts from the *General Directory for Catechesis* Copyright © 1997 Libreria Editrice Vaticana—United States Catholic Conference, Inc. Used with permission. All rights reserved.

*Cover design by Lynn Else*

*Book design by Theresa M. Sparacio*

Copyright © 2002 by Richard Reichert

All rights reserved. No part of this book may be reproduced or transmitted in any form or by any means, electronic or mechanical, including photocopying, recording or by any information storage and retrieval system without permission in writing from the Publisher.

Library of Congress Cataloging-in-Publication Data

Reichert, Ricard.
    Renewing catechetical ministry : a future agenda / Richard Reichert.
        p.   cm.
    Includes bibliographical references.
    ISBN 0-8091-4075-6 (alk. paper)
    1. Catechetics—Catholic Church. 2. Catholic Church—Education. I. Title.

BX1968 .R37 2002
268′.82—dc21

                                                    2002018452

Published by Paulist Press
997 Macarthur Boulevard
Mahwah, New Jersey 07430

www.paulistpress.com

Printed and bound in the
United States of America

# Contents

# Contents

# Abbreviations

| | |
|---|---|
| *AG* | *Ad Gentes,* Second Vatican Council |
| CT | *Catechesi Tradendae* |
| CCC | *Catechism of the Catholic Church* |
| GCD | *General Catechetical Directory* |
| GDC | *General Directory for Catechesis* |
| MPD | *Message to the People of God, Synod of Bishops, 1977* |
| NCCL | National Conference of Catechetical Leadership |
| NCDD | National Conference of Diocesan Directors |
| RCIA | Rite of Christian Initiation of Adults |
| SC | *Constitution on Sacred Liturgy,* Second Vatican Council |
| USCCB | United States Catholic Conference of Bishops |

# Introduction: Promises to Keep

For many of us "old timers" whose catechetical ministry in behalf of the church spans both sides of the Second Vatican Council, that council and the years immediately following it were experienced as a time of great promise for our ministry. Looking back over the decades that have passed since the council, however, it is safe to say that many of those promises we anticipated with such hope and pursued with such enthusiasm continue to elude us. We are not saying that nothing was accomplished during that period Just the opposite. We have made solid progress toward authentic renewal of catechetical ministry. We have laid essential foundations for achieving that renewal. Yet it is one of the basic premises of this book—and the reason for undertaking it—that we are only half way to the completion of our task of renewing catechesis. The much discussed and sought after "paradigm shift" in the way we view and carry out our ministry is yet to be achieved.

On the positive side, precisely because we have made some excellent progress, the other and equally critical premise of this book is that we are now poised to complete our task. That we have reached this point of readiness just as we enter the third millennium is probably more coincidental than causal, since there is no magic per se contained in the act of turning the page on the calendar. But it is our contention that various forces and movements both within the church and in society are converging in the early years of the third millennium, and these are providing our ministry with the important new insights and also with the infusion of renewed energy and enthusiasm required to

1

complete the task begun at Vatican II. Based on these premises, *this book proposes and examines the elements of a rather radical new catechetical agenda for the third millennium,* an agenda that if pursued we are convinced will lead to the desired paradigm shift and to the completion of the task of the renewal of catechesis that Vatican II promised.

## HISTORIC PERSPECTIVE NEEDED

Those too young to remember the initial excitement generated by Vatican II and those who began their catechetical career after its initial impact on the ministry may be puzzled by this call for a new agenda. While granting that there is always need for improvement, they might ask whether expressions like "completing the renewal of catechesis" and talk of a need for a paradigm shift are a little too dramatic or even drastic.

Because they have not personally experienced how much the ministry actually has changed since the days before Vatican II, they are not in a position to appreciate the promise that council contained and thus how far we still have to go to achieve it. They might understandably presume "we've always done it this way" and also presume it is enough to continue in essentially the same manner. Through no fault of their own they are not fully aware of the degree to which the catechetical renewal has stalled and how much radical change is still needed for it to reach the goal envisioned for it by the council.

As is well documented, the Second Vatican Council attempted to identify and strip away various peripheral concepts and practices the church had accumulated over the centuries that were now having the effect of distorting its understanding of its essential nature and distracting it from its essential mission. In the process it called for the church to shed its defensive stance toward society, a stance it had assumed in response to the Protestant Reformation. It directed the church instead to enter into dialogue with that society and to reformulate its message—without compromising it, of course—to make it more understandable to that society.

2

In terms of catechesis we can identify the essential nature of that shift in this way. Prior to the council the goal of catechesis was to help children become loyal, obedient, and conscientious members of the institutional church by providing them with a solid education in the truths of the faith. The council, on the other hand, initiated a shift toward understanding the goal of catechesis as one of forming disciples of Jesus who would be both willing and capable of participating in a community committed to proclaiming and promoting the reign of God in today's society.

This basic thrust of the council had an immediate and radical impact on catechesis. The council called for us to view the faith we were to foster as essentially relational and not just cognitive. That shift required us to reexamine every aspect of our ministry: nature and goals, content or message, methodology, organizational structures and programming, training required of catechists, overall role in the mission of the church, and relationships with the church's other ministries.

These were the tasks we so enthusiastically pursued in the years immediately following the council. Anyone who entered the ministry ten years after the council, therefore, entered a ministry that had already become quite different than it had been in the years just prior to the council. What they cannot recognize, however, is that the thrust and promise for radical renewal provided by the council has in many ways lost its energy and has in fact begun to succumb to subtle forces drawing it away from its understanding of faith as essentially relational and back toward an emphasis on faith as essentially cognitive. In the process there is an equally subtle pressure to readopt the kind of materials, methodology, and program models used in catechesis prior to the council. It is in this historic context that we are advocating the need to pursue energetically the opportunity being provided to us to complete the renewal of catechesis and to effect the promised paradigm shift contained in the council, a shift that embraces not just catechetical goals but ecclesiology. It calls for understanding the church not so much as an institution (although it does of course have an institutional dimension) but as a community of disciples. It therefore calls upon us to move from the goal of educating children to be good members of an institution to the goal of forming all the baptized into disciples of Jesus.

It is our contention that even a casual analysis of our catechetical ministry today will reveal that, despite all the progress made in past decades, it continues to be driven more by the goal of educating good members than forming disciples. It is for that reason that we assert that the renewal of catechesis promised by Vatican II is not yet complete. And it is for that reason we also assert that the very real progress we have been able to make toward that goal is in danger of being lost if we do not seize the opportunity now being given to us to formulate and pursue aggressively an agenda designed to complete that renewal.

## A MODEST PROPOSAL

It would be a presumption bordering on hubris for one person to think he or she can speak for the entire catechetical community and tell it what it must do at the beginning of the third millennium to complete the desired renewal of the ministry. That certainly is not the intention here. Granted, we present by way of a proposal the kind of catechetical agenda we believe is called for at this point in time. But it is offered precisely as that, a proposal we hope the catechetical community will consider. *The overall goal of the book is simply to provide some initial focus and stimulation to the catechetical community in its task of formulating and then pursuing an agenda designed to fulfill the promises contained in Vatican II.*

At this point we need to explain what we mean by the catechetical community, the intended audience for the book. While it may be useful to all of those interested in or involved with catechetical ministry, it is intended especially for those in a position to shape and implement our catechetical agenda. Therefore this catechetical community includes in a special way diocesan directors and their staffs, pastors, directors of religious education (DREs), and principals and their catechetical teams working at

4

the parish level. It includes the members of various catechetical organizations such as the National Conference of Catechetical Leadership. It includes catechetical scholars and theorists in academia, who have always played a critical role in helping shape and give direction to our ministry. It is hoped that ultimately the ideas presented in this book, if not the book itself, will engage the attention of our bishops, who hold ex officio the office of chief catechist in our dioceses.

This much is certain. The catechetical community described above needs to regain the focus, enthusiasm, and momentum it experienced in those years immediately following Vatican II if it is to ever to obtain the promised renewal of its ministry. This requires that it formulate a clear agenda, one supported by a consensus arrived at within the catechetical community itself. As we hope to show, the times are indeed propitious for initiating this next phase in the renewal of catechesis. We presently enjoy a window of opportunity, as it were. But if we fail to act now, this renewal could be set back for another generation or more.

## THE *GENERAL DIRECTORY FOR CATECHESIS*— OUR CATALYST FOR ACTION

As many will recall, just a few years ago the *Catechism of the Catholic Church (CCC)* was heralded as the document that would finally provide the desired cure for all that was perceived as wrong with the church in general and with our catechetical ministry in particular. The document is indeed remarkable and admirable in many ways, but it is safe to say that it has not energized our ministry or the church in the way its advanced billing led us to believe it would. Without intending to be disrespectful, we need to state that the *CCC* of its very nature promotes an understanding of catechesis that has its roots in the pre–Vatican II era and presupposes an ecclesiology rooted in that same era. Embraced uncritically and out of the proper context, it actually threatens to reverse rather than complete the renewal of catechesis begun in Vatican II. (We present a justification of that in appendix 1.)

On the other hand, the *General Directory for Catechesis (GDC)* clearly moves us forward. In many ways it can be considered the single most important catechetical document produced since Vatican II. For that reason it is a premise of this book that the document signals the advent of a new era for catechesis. It can provide both the framework and the momentum we need to complete the renewal. It does not just reiterate the insights of the council and the catechetical documents it generated, such as the *General Catechetical Directory (GCD)*, but actually brings them forward by providing us with new and equally dramatic insights regarding the nature and goal of our ministry. Properly understood it can provide our ministry not just with the guidelines and directions we need to complete our catechetical renewal but also provide us with the authority and courage to pursue our task boldly and with confidence. It is imperative, therefore, that members of the catechetical community rally around the *GDC* and direct their energy to discerning and implementing the initiatives for growth it contains. As we hope to demonstrate in detail in chapter 1, the document gives us the necessary blueprint for identifying and establishing our catechetical agenda for the third millennium. Thus we use it as our basic reference point as we proceed to examine the implications of that agenda throughout the remainder of the book.

The *GDC* requires careful reading and a kind of exegesis. Like most official documents it contains some inherent tensions. It is clear that its authors did not always agree in their approach to catechesis. When the redactors of the Hebrew scriptures could not agree on which version of an event to include in the text, they often compromised by including both. In an analogous way the authors of the *GDC* often compromised and included two sometimes contradictory points of view when they could not agree on which should have priority. In some ways the document reflects the tension between the two opposing understandings of the goal for catechesis mentioned above and the overall tension between the paradigm of church as institution and the paradigm of church as community of disciples. Thus, the insights contained in the document are not always that obvious. A casual reading could lead one to believe the document promotes a "business as usual" approach, which was the impression it initially made on a number of catechists.

## THE PROPOSED AGENDA: AN OVERVIEW

It may be useful here to present a brief overview of the kind of agenda we feel is being generated by the *GDC*, since it can illustrate something of the scope and breadth of what still needs to be done to complete the renewal of catechesis. Though we present this same agenda in more detail in chapter 1, the overview presented here outlines the main topics we explore in the chapters that follow.

One of the document's most significant contributions lies in the clarifications it provides regarding the relationship and interdependence that exist between evangelization and catechesis. It strongly and clearly affirms evangelization as *the* overarching mission of the church. By both demonstrating and stressing the close relationship and interdependence that exists between evangelization and catechesis, the document affirms more forcefully and clearly than all previous catechetical documents the importance and priority status catechesis by nature possesses within the church's overall life and mission. This is the basis for a critical agenda item, namely, the need for our catechetical leadership to advocate effectively for the ministry so that its essential role and importance are once again recognized and adequately supported. We return to this agenda item throughout the book, but it receives special attention in chapters 8 and 9.

Also flowing from this relationship between evangelization and catechesis is another task or agenda item, namely, the need to incorporate the principles of evangelization and what the document refers to as "new evangelization" into our catechesis. This has many implications, especially for catechesis with youth and young adults and for adult catechesis in general. We explore this agenda item especially in chapter 7. The most foundational and consequently critical agenda item, of course, evolves around the need to reclaim formation in discipleship rather than education for membership as the overarching goal and organizational principle for catechesis. That same agenda item calls for us to focus primarily on the relational nature of faith and only secondarily on its cognitive dimension. As stated above, that change in our understanding of the nature of the goal of catechesis in general and the nature of faith in particular is at the core of the paradigm shift initiated by the council, which we seek to complete. If taken seriously, it will alter virtually every aspect of the structure, content, and methodology of our ministry. In particular, it has very important implications for our ability finally to establish adult catechesis as normative and central to ministry without having to sacrifice the attention we now devote to catechesis for children and youth. Given the critical nature of this agenda item for the overall renewal of catechesis, we give it extensive treatment throughout Part I.

Another important agenda item rooted in the *GDC* focuses on the need to revisit and rearticulate our message according to the principles of inculturation. This task, as we hope to demonstrate, goes far beyond the need to be sensitive to ethnic pluralism. It has major implications for how we formulate and present our message in virtually every setting we encounter in today's society. A closely related agenda item suggested by the document involves the need to return to the task of reading the signs of the times, a task that was a strong motivating factor and central concern of Vatican II. If taken seriously, as the *GDC* suggests we need to do, it too will have major implications on the overall shape and content of our message. We deal with these agenda items in chapters 8 and 9.

The role of catechetical leadership in helping the church reclaim the primacy of catechetical ministry emerges as yet another important agenda item. In many ways it is perhaps the most critical from a practical point of view. Unless catechesis is given the full support of the hierarchy and provided both the personnel and financial backing required, the pursuit of the other agenda items and consequent renewal of catechesis cannot hope to succeed. We treat this agenda item in chapter 10.

Finally, though not directly addressed by the document, we need to reexamine the role Catholic schools are to play in catechetical ministry in the third millennium. Though continuing to have great potential as catechetical agents, Catholic schools are nevertheless rather problematic today, given the growing amount of resources they require for their support and the adverse effect this can have on the church's ability to provide resources for other essential ministries. We treat the school-related issues of catechesis in chapter 11.

The above briefly summarizes issues we address in the remainder of the book. Before we continue, however, it is necessary to make a few comments about what to expect. First, much of what follows will have a somewhat familiar ring to veteran catechists. Many of the insights and suggestions given here have been circulating within the catechetical community in one form or another for some time. Yet we are convinced that we will be able to gain a fresh appreciation of them and their true potential for catechetical renewal when they are revisited and properly positioned within the paradigm shift outlined and advocated by the *GDC*. Also, as we will see, many of these "old" ideas are actually like seeds that were planted ahead of their proper growing season; they have lain dormant for a while. Given recent developments and movements both in the church and society, the time is now right for these "seeds" to germinate, take root, and bear fruit.

Second, please keep in mind that the overall intention of the book is to provide a focus and a stimulus for discussion within the catechetical community, one that will lead to the development and adoption of our catechetical agenda for the third millennium. Therefore we treat both the proposed agenda and its practical implications for implementation with broad strokes. *This book is not intended as a detailed "how to" book or a step-by-step manual for renewal of catechesis.* This does not mean that it is entirely lacking in specific suggestions and concrete implications. But it is more like an architect's preliminary sketch than a final blueprint. If the catechetical community comes to consider the sketch acceptable, all of us will then have to share in the task of developing the finished blueprint that can guide us in our renewal of the ministry.

Third, we did not attempt to document our occasional use of information drawn from various studies. We are presuming most readers are already familiar with much of the information we cite and the studies that produced it.

Fourth, at first sight some of the practical suggestions we make regarding how we will have to restructure our content, programs, and methods in the process of implementing the paradigm shift promoted by the *GDC* might seem anything but practical to both our catechetical theorists and to those presently involved "in the trenches." These ideas will undoubtedly evoke some initial reactions like "totally unrealistic," "too naive an approach," or "it will never work," especially from directors and DREs dealing with the real world catechetical issues of parent apathy, the difficulties faced in recruiting volunteer catechists, the lack of support from pastor and parish, the demands already being made on their limited time, their financial resources, and the facilities they have available. This is an understandable reaction. The suggestions made regarding "year round catechesis," for example, will seem foolhardy if viewed within the framework of the current academic paradigm. But any time a true paradigm shift is proposed, it requires that we set aside former ways of defining our goal and approaching our task—including the typical obstacles experienced when using the former approach. Traditional obstacles have a way of disappearing once we move away from traditional definitions and approaches into a new paradigm. To state it another way, perhaps we have failed to grasp the depth, breadth, and radical nature a paradigm shift demands if we measure its validity against how we are accustomed to doing things and the difficulties we face in our present approach. So we ask that readers attempt not to judge our practical suggestions from the old paradigm but rather to view them from within the new paradigm being suggested. Then they might seem much more reasonable.

Finally, the agenda we propose and the issues we consequently explore are not to be considered the only ones contained in the *GDC* nor the only ones the catechetical community can or should address. Ours is not intended as an exhaustive treatment in that sense, nor do we claim to have exhausted all the implications even of the agenda items we do treat. However, we think we have identified the most critical agenda items, those that deserve the catechetical community's most immediate attention. We also believe we have identified the most significant implications that flow from those agenda items.

## CONCLUSION

We hope this introduction adequately explains the nature and intent of the book and the basic premises upon which it rests. We further hope it provides a sense of the scope and parameters of its topic and sets a tone for how we will be dealing with that topic. Finally, we hope it makes clear that our goal has not been to tell the catechetical community what it must do. Rather we hope readers will recognize and accept the invitation it offers to use the ideas presented here solely as a possible basis for discussion and critical dialogue concerning the nature and content of the catechetical agenda in the third millennium.

# PART I
## DISCIPLESHIP—
## THE CENTRAL ISSUE FOR
## RENEWAL OF CATECHESIS

# 1

# A Catechetical Agenda
# for the Third Millennium

## INTRODUCTION: WHERE WE HAVE BEEN

It is safe to say that the church has probably never experienced such a spurt of creativity and renewal of its catechetical ministry as the one that swept over it in the two decades following the Second Vatican Council. This creativity was to a large extent guided by the *GCD,* which was published in 1971. The *GCD,* in turn, was greatly influenced by the insights generated in the now famous International Catechetical Study weeks of the 1960s.

The list of accomplishments during that period is too vast to recount here in its entirety, but we can identify a few of the salient features. The curriculum was carefully adapted, with the help of insights borrowed from the behavioral sciences, to take into account the cognitive and psychological readiness of each age group. Methodology sought to balance the use of inductive and deductive approaches, experience and formal teaching, modern media and traditional text. Fostering a sense of community and providing opportunities for involvement in liturgy and service were integrated into the overall program. There was an explosion in the establishment of top quality catechetical institutes sponsored by various Catholic universities. For almost a generation these programs trained large numbers of catechetical leaders in the latest theological, scriptural, liturgical, and catechetical scholarship. The ministry of the DRE emerged and became firmly rooted in the life of the church. Most of the mainstream textbook series evolved into masterpieces in catechetical pedagogy, reflecting in a responsible way all these new insights in their student materials and teacher guides. In 1972 the Rite of Christian Initiation for Adults (RCIA) was officially declared normative for all catechesis and consequently inspired a new wave of experimentation in alternative program models, materials, and methods.

Despite all the creativity, energy, and dedication of so many catechetical scholars and practitioners for over a generation, the surge of catechetical renewal begun so optimistically after Vatican II seemed to have run its course by the mid 1990s. In view of the increasing numbers of young people who were "dropping out" after being catechized, critics began to question the validity of the catechetical renewal's efforts. It was not uncommon for some of the harshest critics to blame the catechetical renewal for most of the problems the church had begun to experience: the drastic decline in participation in the sacrament of penance and diminishing attendance at the weekend Eucharist; the decline in vocations to priesthood and religious life; the disappearance of traditional devotions, especially those directed to Mary; indifference to the teaching authority of the magisterium; a certain moral laxity, especially in matters related to sexual behavior. Thus, amid these concerns about a lost "Catholic identity" and "theological illiteracy," a catechetical backlash set in. It called for a return to more vigorous teaching of doctrine based on the *Catechism of the Catholic Church (CCC)* and a return to more traditional methods and structures.

We cannot deny the existence of the various problems listed above. And, viewing the situation more than two decades later reveals that mistakes were certainly made in the effort to renew catechesis after Vatican II, especially in the earliest stages of experimentation. But by learning from these early experiences, more valid catechetical insights and innovations were solidly in place by the late 1970s and early 1980s, rooted in sound scholarship, professional leadership, and pastoral dedication. Thus it would be grossly unfair to lay the blame for today's problems exclusively in the lap of the catechetical ministry.

In fact, some do not consider the current difficulties the church experiences to be problems. They prefer to describe them as the inevitable growing pains of a church seeking to transform its ecclesiology from the feudal model of monarchy it adopted in the Middle Ages into the more collegial, communal model called forth by Vatican II. These growing pains are compounded, they observe, by social, political, and cultural upheavals experienced in society as a whole as it struggles to move from an industrial, nationalistic model to a post-industrial, global community.

If one views the church's current difficulties as symptoms in the movement toward a needed transformation—rather than as problems to be solved by reverting to former practices—then it can be argued that the actual effect of the catechetical renewal of the 1970s and 1980s has been to equip those catechized with the theological values and attitudes considered foundational to such a transformation. The *GDC,* the revised version of the earlier *GCD,* describes the accomplishments of the catechetical renewal as follows:

> Catechetical renewal, developed in the Church over the last decades, continues to bear very welcome fruit (cf. *CT* 3, *MPD* 4). The catechesis of children, of young people and of adults has given rise to a type of Christian who is conscious of his faith and who acts consistently with it in his life. In such Christians this catechesis has encouraged:
> • a new and vital experience of God as merciful Father;
> • a more profound discovery of Jesus Christ, not only in his divinity but also in his humanity;
> • a sense of co-responsibility on the part of all for the mission of the Church in the world;
> • and the raising of consciousness with regard to the social obligations of the faith. (art. 24)

These fruits can be considered essential qualities of the kind of faith needed in our time of transition. Awareness of God's loving presence; a reverential intimacy with Jesus; a sensitivity to injustice, oppression, and violence; and a sense of responsibility to serve— what better foundations can one desire if the goal is to renew the church in the modern world?

The *GDC* goes on to describe some of the effects of the Vatican II renewal in general by describing its fruits:

- liturgical life is more profoundly understood as the source and summit of ecclesial life;
- the people of God has acquired a keener awareness of the "common priesthood" (cf. *LG* 10) founded on Baptism and is rediscovering evermore the universal call to holiness and a livelier sense of mutual service in charity;
- the ecclesial community has acquired a livelier sense of the word of God. Sacred Scripture, for example, is read, savored and meditated upon more intensely;
- the mission of the Church in the world is perceived in a new way: on the basis of interior renewal, the Second Vatican Council has opened Catholics to the demands of evangelization as necessarily linked to dialogue with the world, to human development, to different cultures and religions as well as to the urgent quest for Christian unity. (art. 27)

To the degree that the *GDC*'s assessment of these accomplishments is accurate and that we can find these qualities present in most parishes throughout the United States, it is safe to say the efforts of the renewed catechesis have played a critical role in the development of all of them. If the catechesis of the past generation had been the kind of abysmal failure its critics claim, the growth described above simply could not have taken place. Does that mean all is well? Certainly not. The *GDC* cites various catechetical concerns (for example, in articles 25 and 30) and contemporary observers add others worth noting. These include the incursion of secularism and ethical relativism into the ecclesial community, the theological illiteracy and/or imprecision of many adult Catholics, the growing number of disaffected and non-practicing Catholics, especially among young adults and women, the lack of a sense of tradition and of the church's rich history among many of the faithful.

The answer to addressing these very real concerns, however, does not lie in returning to the content and methods of catechesis practiced prior to Vatican II. Rather, it lies in pressing ahead with the catechetical renewal called forth by the council. To guide us in this task we have an invaluable tool, the *GDC*. It is a basic premise of this chapter that the *GDC* is a very providential document and that it holds the key to effecting the next step in the renewal of catechesis—and the church.

## WHERE WE ARE GOING

As a guide to the ongoing renewal of catechesis the *GDC* provides two invaluable services. First, in providing a revision of the original *GCD*, it affirms and brings forward the older document's best and most creative insights. In other words, it continues to build upon that important document's foundations. Second, as one would hope of any revision, it expands upon that foundation by gathering together, clarifying, and setting forth many significant new insights regarding the nature and purpose of catechesis that have emerged since the publication of the *GCD*. It is these new insights we wish to explore here, because they hold the key to guiding us to the next stage of our catechetical renewal. For purposes of clarity we explore these new insights under four broad categories: evangelization, nature and purpose of catechesis, inculturation/adaptation, and context.

### Evangelization

First, the *GDC* does an excellent job of summarizing the most current theological thinking regarding the nature and purpose of evangelization. In the process it clearly identifies evangelization as *the* overarching mission of the church. Second, it does an equally excellent job of clarifying the essential and critical role that catechetical ministry plays in the church's ministry of evangelization. It makes it irrefutably clear that an evangelization unaccompanied and followed by catechesis will be fruitless (see art. 64). This is not a revolutionary or new insight. The original *GCD* made the same observation. However, the expanded treatment of this relationship in the revision is very emphatic in pointing out the absolutely essential role catechesis is called to play in the church's overall mission. This is very timely message, indeed, in an age when dioceses continue to downsize their departments of catechesis and parishes cut their religious education budgets in their efforts to economize.

In addition to stressing (in urgent tones, it can be observed) the close connection between evangelization and catechesis, the revision carefully expands upon and fine tunes the nature of this relationship as originally described in the *GCD*. Put simply, evangelization sows the seed of God's word. Catechesis nurtures its growth through various stages to fruition. Evangelization seeks to proclaim the reality of God's reign made evident in the risen Lord and to invite all people to conversion and discipleship with him. Catechesis gently guides those who respond to this invitation (initial conversion) through various stages of initiation and apprenticeship into the fullness of discipleship. The document then carefully explores the intricate, often overlapping relationship between these two distinct ministries.

## Nature and Purpose of Catechesis

In article 41 the *GDC* describes in very simple terms the goal of catechesis: "It is the task of catechesis to show who Jesus Christ is, his life and ministry, and to present the Christian faith as the following of his person" (cf. *CT* 5; *CCC* 520 and 2053). The document expands on the nature of the faith that catechesis is to foster:

> The Christian faith is, above all, conversion to Jesus Christ (cf. *AG* 13a), full and sincere adherence to his person and the decision to walk in his footsteps (cf. *CT* 5b). Faith is *a personal encounter* [emphasis added] with Jesus Christ, making of oneself a disciple of him. This demands a permanent commitment to think like him, to judge like him and to live as he lived (cf. *CT* 20b). In this way the believer unites himself to the community of disciples and appropriates the faith of the Church (cf. *CCC* 166-167). (art. 53)

By borrowing from and frequently directly quoting from pre-vious documents, the *GDC* puts great emphasis on discipleship throughout its entirety. For example, it quotes from *Catechesi Tradendae* when it states: "The definitive aim of catechesis is to put people not only in touch, but also in communion and inti-macy, with Jesus Christ" (*CT* 5, art. 80). Viewed alone, the idea that catechesis is by nature Christocentric and that its goal is to foster discipleship can hardly be considered new. It is as old as Christianity itself. And we find it stated in all contemporary cate-chetical documents. What is new is the fact that the previous efforts of catechetical renewal have prepared us to take the full significance of this insight seriously. Appreciating and acting upon the real implications of the understanding of the catechetical goal as fostering "communion and intimacy with Jesus Christ" (cf. *CT* 5) is the key to our next stage of catechetical renewal.

This treatment of the purpose of catechesis by the *GDC* points to and encourages a radical shift in how we are to approach the ministry, a shift that affects in a equally radical way both its content and its methods. Stated another way, the *GDC* calls for and encourages a continuation of the catecheti-cal renewal that focuses first of all on developing good Chris-tians or disciples of Jesus. Fostering this commitment to be disciples of Jesus is our first task and is at the core of Catholic identity. Such a commitment to discipleship is the needed lens through which an individual can begin truly to see, understand, appreciate, and embrace all the beliefs and practices contained in the Catholic tradition.

This becomes more clear when we consider how the document describes the process or necessary stages of catechesis. Reaffirming the insights of the catechetical congresses of the 1960s and drawing on the stages of initiation set forth in the RCIA, the *GDC* speaks of three distinct stages of gradual growth. There is *pre-catechesis,* described as a proclamation of the gospel that "shall always be done in close connection with human nature and its aspirations, and will show how the Gospel fully satisfies the human heart" (art. 117; also cf. *AG* 8a). Then there is *initiatory catechesis,* described as

21

"the period in which conversion to Jesus Christ is formalized, and provides a basis for first adhering to him. Converts, by means of 'a period of formation, an apprenticeship in the whole Christian life' (cf. *AG* 14), are initiated into the mystery of salvation and an evangelical style of life" (art. 63). The *GDC* further describes the characteristics of this central and most critical stage of catechesis by stating that "it is an apprenticeship in the entire Christian life, it is a 'complete Christian initiation' (*CT* 21), which promotes an authentic following of Christ, focused on his Person" (art. 67). It also states, "As it is formation for the Christian life it comprises but surpasses mere instruction (cf. *CT* 33 and *CCC* 1231; *AG* 14). Being essential, it looks to what is 'common' for the Christian, without entering into disputed questions nor transforming itself into a form of theological investigation" (art. 68).

The document also speaks of the period or stage of continuing or *permanent catechesis,* designed for those who have been apprenticed and initiated into the life of discipleship and the community of disciples. In Article 71 it lists the many forms of this ongoing catechesis available through the normal pastoral activity of the church. For example, it cites participation in the liturgy and the homily, scripture study, spiritual formation activities, occasional catechesis on a particular topic, formal theological instruction, and so forth.

Finally the *GDC* makes a very important point when it recognizes that:

> Frequently, many who present themselves for catechesis truly require genuine conversion....Only by starting with conversion, and therefore by making allowance for the interior disposition of "whoever believes" can catechesis, strictly speaking fulfill its proper task of education in the faith. (art. 62; cf. RCIA 9, 10, 50; *CT* 19)

We will attempt shortly to identify the practical implications the above points stressed by the *GDC* have for catechetical renewal. First, however, we need to describe briefly the two other key insights of the document, namely, inculturation/adaptation and context.

## Inculturation/Adaptation

In its efforts to renew its mission of evangelization the church has given special attention in recent decades to the concept and importance of inculturation. Given the close connection the *GDC* establishes between evangelization and catechesis, it is not surprising that the document also gives special attention to the role of inculturation and its implications for catechesis. It details these in particular in Articles 109–10, but the theme runs throughout the document. Stated simply, the principle of inculturation calls upon us to discern, respect, and then build upon those values already present in a culture that are compatible with the gospel and God's reign. At the same time we need to be ready to challenge those who stand in opposition to it.

Adaptation, though similar, calls on us to adopt the language, imagery, and methods that are most capable of rendering the gospel message understandable and acceptable to those in the cultural or age group to whom we proclaim it. If music is valued by a particular age or ethnic group, then we need to adapt our methodology accordingly. When speaking of the need for adaptation in catechizing youth, for example, the *GDC* states:

> One of the difficulties to be addressed and resolved is the question of "language" *(mentality, sensibility, tastes, style, vocabulary)* between young people and the Church *(catechesis, catechists)*. A necessary "adaptation of catechesis to young people" is urged, in order to translate into their terms "the message of Jesus with patience and wisdom and without betrayal." (art. 185; cf. *CT* 40)

The concepts of inculturation and adaptation are not new. They can be found in the original *GCD* and other earlier catechetical documents. What *is* new and hence noteworthy is the increased degree of importance the *GDC* gives to them.

## Context

Culture refers to those deep-seated values and philosophical constructs embedded in a group's collective psyche. For example, it is often said that the value we place on individualism is a defining element in the American psyche and hence the American culture. Context, on the other hand, is akin to what is more often referred to as the "signs of the times." Though the *GDC* does not treat the role of context as a separate topic, it does make specific reference to the importance of reading the "signs of the times" (see art. 31–32, 39, 108).

Thus, context or the "signs of the times" embraces the more temporal conditions and circumstances affecting people's thinking and behavior at a particular time. The impact the Internet is having on our society, the role the media now play in our lives and in our decision making, the growing prevalence of single-parent families and of families in which both parents work outside the home, the impact of the feminist movement, the growing gap between rich and poor, the increase in fundamentalist movements—these are all examples of context in which we are called to minister.

On the topic of context the document teaches more by example than by providing any new insights regarding its importance for ministry. In various places the document provides an accurate and often painfully honest analysis of the kinds of problems present today within the church and within society. In doing so, the document makes it clear that to minister effectively we need to read the "signs of the times" carefully.

## IMPLICATIONS FOR THE CATECHETICAL AGENDA

By drawing out the implications of the major insights of the *GDC* we just reviewed, we can discern the essential elements or pillars of the next stage in the renewal of catechesis. They make up the basis for the catechetical agenda for the third millennium. We can only summarize them here but will explore each more fully in later chapters.

### Catechesis as Essential Ministry

Fundamental to the continuing renewal of catechesis is the need to reclaim its privileged status as an essential ministry of the church, integral to the success of the church's overarching mission to evangelize. In recent years catechesis has been downplayed and downsized. Facing the need to economize, many dioceses have chosen to do so at the expense of their catechetical offices. In similar circumstances many parishes have chosen to turn to less expensive (and often less qualified) volunteers to lead their catechetical programs rather than continue to employ full-time and degreed or certified DREs. Reversing this trend, one that is snowballing, will be no easy task. In our very human church, economic realities too often take precedence over theological ones. There is today a critical need for a major, concerted effort by catechetical leaders at every level—national, diocesan, and parish—to initiate dialogue with our institutional leaders over this issue. It seems of late that our catechetical leaders have too often assumed a defensive, apologetic stance. Just as often they have failed to recognize the very real success of their efforts to date and/or have failed to speak boldly enough of the essential importance and dignity of their ministry.

It is to be hoped that, bolstered by the example of the *GDC*, which speaks quite clearly of the success catechesis has had to date and even more forcefully about its essential importance for the overall vitality and mission of the church in the future, catechetical leaders will find both the rationale and the motivation to reclaim the ministry's rightful place and priority in the life of the church. This is a foundational task for the continuation of catechetical renewal. The development of concrete leadership strategies for carrying out that task should have a central place in catechetical agenda for the third millennium.

## Nature and Purpose of Catechesis

Here we are at the core of the agenda for continuing the renewal. As noted above, regarding the nature and purpose of catechesis the *GDC* (art. 80), quoting from *CT*, states:

> The definitive aim of catechesis is to put the person not only in touch, but also in communion and intimacy, with Jesus Christ. (*CT* 5)

25

It also states:

The Christian faith is, above all, conversion to Jesus Christ (cf. *AG* 13a), full and sincere adherence to his person and the decision to walk in his footsteps (cf. *CT* 5b). Faith is *a personal encounter* [emphasis added] with Jesus Christ, making of oneself a disciple of him. (art. 53)

Finally it states:

Frequently, many who present themselves for catechesis truly require genuine conversion....Only by starting with conversion, and therefore by making allowance for the interior disposition of "whoever believes," can catechesis, strictly speaking, fulfill its proper task of education in the faith. (art. 62; cf. RCIA 9, 10, 50; *CT* 19)

The shift implied here is critical. For too long too much of our catechesis has moved too quickly over the task of establishing an intimate relationship with Jesus, of providing a "personal encounter." Put simply, too often and for too long we have presumed a conversion that was not there and launched into what is more properly considered continuing or permanent catechesis. In another era, when the gospel dominated a particular culture, the parish played a central role in a person's life, and intact families played a major role in fostering the faith of their children, such a presumption was valid. But those conditions began to disintegrate over forty years ago.

The *GDC* is quite emphatically calling upon us to focus once again not just on a theology about Jesus but on the person of Jesus. It is calling upon us to focus once again on the initial task of nurturing a conversion to his person and to discipleship before attempting to present in detail all the implications, theological subtleties, and ecclesial traditions entailed in a life of discipleship. We need to focus on initiation into discipleship rather than on more advanced catechetical topics. The *GDC* characterizes very well what is to be presented during this initiation when it states that "it looks to what is 'common' for the Christian, without

entering into disputed questions nor transforming itself into a
form of theological investigation." (art. 68)

In this light the catechetical agenda for the third millennium
needs to deal with questions such as these:

- How can we shape our catechesis so that it addresses the
  very real and ongoing need for initial conversion in the
  children, youth, and adults to whom we minister? In other
  words, how do we make pre-catechesis a more integral
  and enduring part of our ministry?
- How must we adapt our catechesis so that it truly focuses on
  fostering an encounter with the person of Jesus and on fostering the experience of intimacy and communion with him?
- In this light (of fostering intimacy with Jesus) to what
  extent do we need to simplify the content of our message
  and therefore reexamine the nature and content of the
  texts and by extension the methods we use?
- What implications does this have for how we structure our
  programs? Is the classroom model still to be used? If so,
  how must it be adapted? If not, what other alternatives are
  possible? What is the proper role of the parish and of the
  family in fostering this kind of intimacy with Jesus and
  providing an apprenticeship for budding disciples?
- What implications do the above have for how we train
  catechists? for the qualifications and job description of the
  future DRE?

In short, if we are to take the *GDC*'s analysis of the nature
and purpose of catechesis seriously, we are being asked to reexamine every aspect of how we presently do catechesis.

## Inculturation/Adaptation

To date our catechesis has acknowledged in theory the
importance of the principles of inculturation and adaptation. The
catechetical agenda for the third millennium demands that we
now apply them vigorously. We need to make a concerted effort to

discern the nature and extent a particular culture is in fact exerting on those we catechize—its positive influences and the obstacles it presents to conversion and growth in discipleship. We need to adapt our message and methods not just in terms of stages of psychological readiness but also in terms of how the culture is influencing that readiness.

This is no easy task, especially in a pluralistic or multicultural society such as the United States. We need to look for starters to current scholarship in sociology and cultural anthropology; and research in the nature and effect of symbol, ritual and myth, ethnology and ethics, and the role of art and music.

In short, we possess a gospel whose language and imagery has been shaped by a Mediterranean, Near-Eastern culture over two thousand years ago. We have a Catholic tradition predominately shaped by and filtered through the experience of a Western European culture. How can we fashion and present this message in the third millennium so that it remains authentic and is also both understandable and appealing to those living in today's pluralistic, post-industrial, and uniquely American culture? The continuation of catechetical renewal depends in large extent on our ability to answer that question.

## Context

This is an equally challenging item on the agenda for the ongoing renewal of catechesis in the third millennium. It calls upon us to read the "signs of the times," trying to discern which contemporary movements, trends, and events reveal the presence and action of the Spirit. By recognizing such signs we can take full advantage of the resulting receptivity to the gospel that the Spirit is cultivating in those we hope to catechize. What makes this task challenging is the fact that many "signs of the times" reflect the parable of wheat and weeds. The good is tinged by potential harm. For example, that there is a growing hunger for spirituality in today's society is a positive sign. It is clearly of the Spirit. At the same time, this hunger is making many people vulnerable to superficial pietism, to rigid fundamentalism, or to ancient superstitious practices newly disguised as authentic spirituality. The Internet can be viewed as such a "sign of the times," since it can be a powerful tool for fostering communication and growth in mutual understanding. But social critics observe it can also isolate and dehumanize its users. These examples illustrate our need as catechists to be very circumspect and to call upon the wisdom of the whole community in our efforts at discernment. Only then can we hope to avoid the trap of fadism in our catechesis, a trap into which we too often fell in our earliest efforts at renewal shortly after Vatican II.

Another equally challenging aspect of this task is the fact that we must apply the same discernment to events and trends not just in society but within the ecclesial community. What is the current crisis in vocations and the priest shortage telling us? What are we to make of the large numbers of Catholics, especially among young and middle-aged adults, who are turning to other Christian churches to be nurtured? How are we to view the increasing tension that is gathering around the issue of the proper role of women in the church? We need to discern carefully the potential meaning contained in these and many other experiences and movements within the contemporary church. What might the Spirit be trying to tell us as a church and how should that affect the shaping of our catechetical message, structures, and methods? This too is a critical item on our catechetical agenda.

## CONCLUSION

We have proposed that the catechetical renewal initiated by Vatican II, though fruitful, was just the first stage in a long-term renewal process. We have further proposed that, motivated and guided by the insights of the *GDC*, we are now called to enter a new stage in this ongoing process. We have also proposed that the elements of the agenda for that renewal process can be found through a careful reading of the document. Finally, we have identified and described in a preliminary way this catechetical agenda for the third millennium. This brief analysis by no means exhausts the riches of the document. It clearly contains many other implications from which we can develop other important agenda items. We believe, however, that the above items deserve our most immediate attention, and it is these agenda items, and corollary agenda items that flow from them, that we explore in the remainder of the book.

# 2

# Developing a Catechesis
# of Discipleship

## INTRODUCTION

Of the various items of the catechetical agenda for the third millennium proposed in this chapter, the need to develop a catechesis of discipleship is the linchpin. The importance and effectiveness of the others depend on the success we have in completing a paradigm shift in how we understand and do catechesis. We examine some of the most important implications of such a shift in this chapter.

## CLARIFYING THE PROBLEM

The following quotations from the *GDC* help put the issue in context:

> The definitive aim of catechesis is to put people not only in touch, but also in communion and intimacy, with Jesus Christ. (*CT* 5) (art. 80)

> The Christian faith is, above all, conversion to Jesus Christ (cf. *AG* 13), full and sincere adherence to his person and the decision to walk in his footsteps (cf. *CT* 5b). Faith is a personal encounter with Jesus Christ, making of oneself a disciple of him. This demands a permanent commitment to think like him, to judge like him and to live as he lived (cf. *CT* 20b). In this way the believer unites himself to the community of

disciples and appropriates the faith of the Church. (Cf. CCC 166-167) (art. 53)

[Initiatory catechesis is] the period in which conversion to Jesus Christ is formalized, and provides the basis for first adhering to him. Converts, by means of "a period of forma-tion, an apprenticeship in the whole Christian life" (*AG* 14), are initiated into the mystery of salvation and an evangelical style of life. (art. 63)

Though the precise wording may vary, these quotes from the *GDC* echo and in some instances directly quote from all the ear-lier catechetical documents such as *Catechesi Tradendae* in stating that the goal of catechesis is to bring people into communion with our Lord, Jesus Christ as disciples. If this is such a well-established fact, one might rightly ask, "Just what is the problem?"

Perhaps an example can help illustrate the "problem." A psy-chologist friend of mine is an avowed member of the Jungian school of psychology, a loyal and vocal disciple of Carl Jung. As a graduate student she read everything Jung wrote and much of what has been written about his work. She now applies his princi-ples of psychology faithfully (and with much success) in her prac-tice. She has defended his theories with vigor and intelligence in papers and seminars in response to colleagues who have chal-lenged them. One could say she is "in communion" with Jung or "believes in Jung." Yet she has never implied that she has any kind of *personal relationship* with him. She doesn't attempt, for exam-ple, to converse with him in prayer. I do not believe she even has a picture of him in her office or home. Others rightly can be described as disciples of other great thinkers: Einstein, Darwin, and even some diehard disciples of Marx and Lenin. Yet none can be said to have (or aspire to form) a personal relationship with their deceased teacher.

The point, though perhaps not obvious, is important. Have we as catechists unintentionally been fostering this kind of disci-pleship with Jesus? Have we been spending more time handing down a "school of thought" about Jesus and his teachings than we have in nurturing an intimate personal friendship with Jesus?

Have we been looking at discipleship (communion with or belief in Jesus) more as a description of doctrinal orthodoxy than as a description of a personal relationship of affectionate intimacy, total trust, and mutual self-donation?

Any catechists who have been in the trenches since shortly after Vatican II will probably bristle at the mere suggestion. Perhaps the most significant change in catechesis after the council has been the ongoing effort to promote a biblical understanding of faith as a dynamic personal relationship with God, a personal response to God's invitation to covenantal friendship. The dominate theme of catechesis, the veterans will point out, has been the attempt to move away from rote teaching of the truths of our faith that marked the era before Vatican II toward fostering this more biblical, personal faith that is rooted in and flows from one's life experiences. Agreed. But what catechists have failed to realize is just how difficult it is to effect such a change. Two generations of this renewed approach to catechesis is not much time when set beside the previous 450 years (more than twenty generations).

Catechesis during those centuries was geared toward protecting the flock first from Protestantism and then from a whole series of other "isms"—rationalism, nationalism, liberalism, modernism, higher criticism, communism, etc.—that marched through Europe in the eighteenth, nineteenth, and early twentieth centuries. It would not be fair to fault the church for assuming a defensive stance and mentality; its very existence was being threatened by some of these movements. Nor did the church during that time ignore the importance of one's personal relationship to Jesus. Yet a kind of catechetical dichotomy did develop during that time which I contend continues to some degree to shape our catechetical thinking and practice to this day—the Vatican II renewal notwithstanding. Namely, catechesis began to focus almost exclusively on handing down orthodox beliefs. One's personal relationship to God (biblical faith) became just that, a personal matter to be fostered through the sacramental life and the wide variety of private devotions and devotional practices that abounded in the church.

33

Thus for over four hundred years catechesis focused primarily on handing down a belief system, a body of truths about Jesus, his teachings, and the church he established. In the process it began to speak in terms more proper to (religious) education than to catechesis and gradually adopted schooling models as its primary methodology. It presumed (sometimes rightly, sometimes wrongly) that those being catechized already possessed a personal faith in Jesus that was being nurtured by their personal participation in the sacramental and devotional life of the church.

Therefore, even though today's catechists have enthusiastically embraced the ideal and the rhetoric of a holistic catechesis designed to foster personal discipleship, in actual practice we have not succeeded in effecting the required paradigm shift. Both our materials and our methods continue to reflect the dichotomized approach to discipleship just described. Catechesis continues to be dominated by various forms of the schooling models we inherited, and we continue to direct most of our energy to handing down a school of thought about Jesus, his teachings, and his church.

Granted, much has been done to provide a more integrated or holistic catechesis that seeks to balance the teaching of formal content with experiences of prayer and sacrament, the building of community, and opportunities for service. The RCIA, officially considered the normative form of catechesis, clearly reflects the desired paradigm shift. Though admittedly flawed and not always practical, the lectionary model has been another attempt. Some confirmation programs for older youth come close to a truly holistic catechesis. I have also seen some wonderful local programs in individual parishes throughout the country. But they tend to be just that, localized exceptions to the rule, for the most part unrepeatable because they depend on the personal charisms of some particularly gifted local DREs and catechists. Also, attempts to involve parents and the community as partners in catechesis reflect this awareness that catechesis is about more than teaching the faith. To a large extent, however, we have yet to overcome the dichotomized approach to discipleship that we inherited. Too often, any efforts to foster discipleship precisely as a personal relationship with Jesus tend to be treated as enrichment, something added on to the core program, namely, the *religious education* program.

A simple glance at the scope and sequence of most published curriculum programs, whether those developed by diocesan offices or those developed by textbook publishers, illustrates the problem. Given the limited amount of time catechists can spend with the children and youth, either in a day-school program or a parish (CCD) program, the amount of material to present in a given year can seem overwhelming. If catechists are expected to deal with all that material (and they are), no wonder they are hesitant to spend too much time on activities that are not clearly related to the expressed content of the curriculum. In other words, it is not the person of Jesus but our curriculums that tend to drive our catechesis. And to a large extent these curriculums continue to reflect the concern that began during the Reformation to hand down all the basic truths of the faith.

It should not be surprising to find that this concern for transmitting an orthodox and comprehensive body of truths, having dominated catechesis for the past 450 years, now seems deeply rooted in our collective catechetical psyche. Try as we may, it is difficult for us to imagine any other way of doing catechesis. The dedicated catechists who have been struggling to effect a renewal of the ministry might in some ways be compared to the mythological character Sisyphus, who was condemned each day to push a huge boulder up a steep mountain, only to find the boulder back at the bottom of the slope the next morning. The force of 450 years of "catechetical gravity" seems to be working against us.

Nor does the present atmosphere within the official church help. Its preoccupation with preserving orthodoxy and its sometimes heavy-handed way of going about the task (the loyalty oath, the silencing of various theologians, and so on) only serve to reinforce the notion that orthodoxy and comprehensiveness should be the main concerns of catechesis. The CCC is in many ways a marvelous document, but the timing and the motivation behind its publication also have had the effect of reinforcing the notion that the primary role of catechesis is to transmit an

35

orthodox and comprehensive body of truths. And the norms and methods used by the U.S. Bishops' Office for the Catechism in evaluating religious education textbooks tends to have the same effect. Much of the discussion today about having lost our Catholic identity is centered on the need to restore orthodoxy and comprehensiveness to our catechesis.

We need to state clearly here that we are not opposed to orthodoxy and comprehensiveness when it comes to transmitting the truths revealed by God through Jesus and reflected upon by the church over the past two thousand years. We view the transmission of these truths as a legitimate catechetical task. In saying that we need to rethink the goal of catechesis, our concern is more with priorities, with the fact that as catechesis is presently practiced the tail seems to be wagging the dog.

## CATECHESIS OF DISCIPLESHIP

How do we overcome the effects of the "catechetical gravity" described above and make the shift to the catechesis of discipleship initiated by Vatican II and promoted in all the ensuing catechetical documents, especially the *GDC*? That is the question we wish to explore in this chapter. We feel such a catechesis of discipleship has three interrelated and often overlapping dimensions: catechesis as encounter, catechesis as apprenticeship, and catechesis as initiation into the community of disciples.

### Catechesis as Encounter

The *GDC* describes discipleship with Jesus as the "permanent commitment to think like him, to judge like him and to live as he lived. In this way the believer unites himself to the community of disciples and appropriates the faith of the Church" (art. 53; also cf. *CT* 20b and *CCC* 166–167). This kind of commitment presupposes an initial act of faith, a self-donation to the person of Jesus. The source of such faith, as pointed out in article 53 of the *GDC* "is a personal encounter with Jesus Christ."

36

If the faith upon which discipleship rests comes from personal encounter with Jesus, it takes no special leap in logic to recognize that the foundational task of catechesis is to provide opportunities for such a personal encounter. It is our premise that providing such ongoing opportunities to encounter Jesus is also the first and most fundamental challenge we face in our attempt to complete the catechetical renewal initiated by Vatican II. All else we strive to achieve through our catechesis depends upon and flows from the success we have in accomplishing that foundational task.

Before we can examine the practical implications this premise has on our catechetical methods and structures, we must first clarify the nature of the desired encounter itself. The *GDC* speaks of the need "to put the person not only in touch, but also in communion and intimacy, with Jesus Christ" (art. 80, cited from *CT* 5). An encounter, then, can be described as an opportunity to be "in touch with" Jesus. The goal of such an encounter is to deepen one's personal relationship with Jesus. Put very simply, catechesis as encounter means providing such *opportunities* to be "in touch with" and to get to know Jesus better at the personal level. In seeking to provide these opportunities, we need to respect certain principles that are at play.

First, in many instances these opportunities will need to contain elements of evangelization, what the *GDC* describes as new evangelization (arts. 58–59). This applies especially in those cases where

> many who present themselves for catechesis truly require genuine conversion. Because of this the Church usually desires that the first stage in the catechetical process be dedicated to ensuring conversion (cf. *CT* 19; *GCD* 18)....In the context of "new evangelization" it is effected by means of a "kerygmatic catechesis," sometimes called a "pre-catechesis."...Only by starting with conversion, and therefore by making allowance for the interior disposition of "whoever believes" can catechesis, strictly speaking, fulfill its proper task of education in the faith. (Cf. RCIA 9, 10, 50; *CT* 19) (art. 62)

The situation just cited describes a significant number of those in catechetical programs today. Though baptized and having an identification with the church, their personal relationship to Jesus and their knowledge about him, his teachings, and his ministry are rudimentary at best. Often their information is tinged by half-truths and pious notions that actually serve as obstacles to any desire to draw close to him in friendship. Thus, our efforts to provide opportunities for encounter often will require us to use principles of evangelization to be effective. Specifically, this means catechesis will often have to devote considerable time and energy to fostering those inner dispositions of openness and attentiveness required before any personal encounter with another can be experienced.

Second, the *GDC* wisely states that we will need to apply the principles of *kerygmatic catechesis* in our efforts to provide opportunities for encountering the risen Lord. That is, we will have to spend much of our time simply telling the story. However, since many of those we catechize come to us with half-truths and pious notions about the story, we must be able to present it in ways that allow them to hear the gospel again for the first time, so to speak. In this context many of the principles of inculturation and adaptation come into play as we shape our message.

Third, the task of providing opportunities to get to know Jesus better at the personal level necessitates a continual *process*. It is not something we do in a particular grade or in a particular lesson. It must be an integral part of our catechesis each time we gather—until those we catechize are firmly rooted (initiated) in discipleship and in the life of the community of disciples.

The fourth principle follows from the third. Because opportunities for encounter should be provided continually throughout this initiatory phase of catechesis, they will need to be *progressive*, carefully adapted to psychological and intellectual capacities of the various age groups. Simply stated, we will have to adjust and tailor our opportunities for encounter to the readiness of the group we catechize.

The fifth and perhaps most challenging principle to be applied when approaching catechesis as encounter is that of *sacramentality*.

We are striving to put people in touch with the risen Lord—invisible, existing beyond the realm of our senses. Our primary access to the risen Lord is through prayer and through those signs that reveal his presence and action to us, both of which presume a basic faith. Faith is a gift of the Spirit over which we have no ultimate control. But through our catechesis we can foster both prayer and sacramental sensitivity—an understanding of the nature of signs and an openness and alertness to those signs by which the risen Lord reveals himself to us. Developing this prayerfulness and sacramental sensitivity is an essential aspect of catechesis as encounter.

Keeping these principles in mind, we want to turn briefly to the chief means catechists have at their disposal for providing ongoing opportunities to be in touch with and to get to know Jesus better at the personal level. The three most essential ones are word, witness, and prayer. We can provide a kind of direct access to Jesus through scripture, especially the gospels when presented in a kerygmatic manner. The witness of other disciples, individually and as a community, living and dead, has a sacramental quality that can also reveal the presence and action of Jesus in our midst. The role of the catechist as such a witness, a living sacrament, is especially important. Finally, catechesis as encounter takes place whenever we provide an atmosphere or ambiance of prayerfulness. The very act of coming together should have the effect of creating a sacred space or holy ground. The time together needs to be approached and developed as a prayerful time, a holy time, an ecclesial action akin to Eucharist.

We will explore some of practical implications of these means for engendering encounter when we deal more specifically with the methodology called forth by a catechesis of discipleship. Now, however, we want to examine the second aspect of such catechesis, namely, catechesis as apprenticeship.

## Catechesis as Apprenticeship

As mentioned, catechesis as encounter is an ongoing process intended to awaken and then deepen the individual's desire, motivation, and commitment to follow Jesus. As the *GDC* states, this is a "commitment to think like him, to judge like him and to live as he lived" (art. 53; cf. *CT* 20b). Catechesis as apprenticeship, therefore, seeks to build upon this desire, motivation, and commitment by presenting and developing the knowledge and skills required to live out one's discipleship.

The tasks of a disciple involve three related activities:

- To walk with, follow along with, or be a companion of Jesus, our Lord and friend (commitment to him)
- To learn from Jesus, our Master (to think and judge like him)
- To participate in the mission and ministry of Jesus, our Savior (to act like him)

Catechesis as apprenticeship focuses on gradually helping the individual acquire the knowledge and skills needed to carry out these three tasks. Such an apprenticeship involves both instruction and opportunities to exercise the required skills. The three tasks, therefore, become the framework for developing the catechetical curriculum, or the content of a catechesis of discipleship. The relevance of the content is determined by how useful it is helping individuals better walk with, think like, and act in partnership with Jesus. We will explore the practical implications catechesis as apprenticeship has on the development of our overall catechetical curriculum in the next chapter.

## Catechesis as Initiation

Immediately after describing discipleship as the permanent "commitment to think like him, to judge like him and to live as he lived" (art. 53; cf. *CT* 20b), the *GDC* goes on to say: "In this way the believer unites himself to the community of disciples and appropriates the faith of the Church" (cf. *CCC* 166–167). The document is simply emphasizing the accepted fact that Christian discipleship is not intended as a private matter. Rather, it is a public act that establishes the individual in a vital and intimate relationship with the visible community of disciples, the church.

Thus the third aspect of a catechesis of discipleship involves the gradual initiation of each disciple into the life of the church so he or she can in due time discover the fullness of its teachings and traditions, enter enthusiastically into its sacramental rituals, and participate responsibly in its mission and ministries. The community (which includes both the domestic church or family and the local church or parish) is at once the locus toward which initiation aims and an active participant in the initiatory process.

The role of the community is to be modeled after the role the RCIA team and sponsors play in leading adult converts to full initiation into the community. As such, the community is called upon to give ongoing witness of what it means to be disciples as well as provide a sacramental sign of the presence and action of Jesus in its midst. The community is called upon to mentor and journey with the budding disciples, sharing with them the wisdom of its tradition and guiding them in their efforts to carry out the tasks of discipleship. Finally, the community provides the locus and opportunity for disciples to experience its lived tradition, to participate in its rituals and symbols, and to begin to share in its mission and ministry. It is the duty of the community's catechists to develop their formal catechetical program to facilitate and ensure this interaction between the catechized and the community.

The above description may seem somewhat idealistic, but it nevertheless accurately depicts the scope and critical importance the community plays in catechesis as initiation. Just as evangelization will remain fruitless if unaccompanied by catechesis, so even the best catechetical program is rendered fruitless in the absence of a welcoming and supportive initiatory community. It is safe to say that ongoing renewal of catechesis is dependent to a large extent on our ability to help the domestic church (family) and the local church (parish community) recognize themselves as a community of disciples and to assume their critical roles in the catechesis of discipleship, especially the initiatory aspect of that catechesis just described. This, in turn, underscores the importance of the first agenda item we identified earlier, namely, the need for catechetical leaders to strive to reestablish catechesis in its essential and pivotal role in the life of the church.

This overview of catechesis as initiation serves only to illustrate what catechesis entails in general terms. The implications contained in this overview, however, are far reaching and, as indicated, critical to the overall success of the catechetical ministry and its ongoing renewal.

## CONCLUSION

In attempting to describe the nature of the proposed catechesis of discipleship we have identified its three distinct but closely interrelated aspects: catechesis as encounter; catechesis as apprenticeship; and catechesis as initiation. An ongoing catechesis of encounter continually inspires and deepens one's commitment to be a disciple. This growing commitment in turn provides the prerequisite rationale and motivation for participating in catechesis as apprenticeship. Apprenticeship, in turn, needs to take place within and is oriented toward the community—its life of fellowship, ritual celebration, and mission.

A catechesis of discipleship, then, requires the presence and ongoing interplay of each of these three aspects to be effective. It is these same three aspects that we find in the first school of discipleship, the gospel. The first disciples encountered and deepened their relationship with Jesus in daily interaction. Through regular instruction and "practice missions" Jesus provided their apprenticeship, an apprenticeship experienced in a community with its ongoing demands for cooperation, forbearance, selflessness, mutual support, and humility.

It is our conviction that the catechetical renewal begun with Vatican II laid the foundations for the development of such a catechesis of discipleship within the church. The *GDC* provides the guidance and encouragement to carry this renewal process to its completion. We look with hope to its unfolding in the third millennium.

# 3

# The Content of a Catechesis of Discipleship

## INTRODUCTION

In our traditional understanding of catechesis we have tended to think of content primarily as a curriculum—a body of information and skills to be pursued through a formal, systematic course of study. To a certain degree one can measure outcomes after pursuing such a course by means of objective testing. But if we begin to understand the nature and purpose of catechesis in terms of discipleship, a shift occurs in how we think of content. As the *GDC* states, "The concept of catechesis which one has, profoundly conditions the selection and organization of its contents *(cognitive, experiential, behavioral)*" (art. 35).

As mentioned above, there are three distinct aspects to the catechesis of discipleship: encounter, apprenticeship, and initiation. Though closely linked and interdependent, each has its own proper content. The proper content or focus of catechesis understood as encounter, for example, is the person of Jesus. Thus, in catechesis as encounter the goal is to provide opportunities for those catechized to get to *know Jesus better* by experiencing his presence and action in their lives. In a similar way, the proper content or focus of catechesis understood as initiation is essentially the local community of disciples. In catechesis as initiation the goal is to provide opportunities for those catechized to get to *know the community better* by experiencing and participating in its lived faith and living tradition, its symbols and ritual celebrations, its mission and ministries. It is obvious that such content is essentially experiential. Neither is it easily shaped into a body of information and skills to be pursued through a formal, systematic course of study, one that measures outcomes through some form of objective testing.

When we approach catechesis as apprenticeship, however, its proper content does come closer to our traditional understanding of a curriculum. Therefore, it is in terms of apprenticeship that we will be exploring the proper content of the catechesis of discipleship in this chapter. In such a "curriculum of apprenticeship" there is a definite body of factual information to be acquired, truths to be grasped, skills to be developed, and attitudes to be fostered. Also, this content can be systematically organized around particular themes, much like a traditional curriculum. But certain principles are at work in the shaping of the content proper to apprenticeship that render it quite distinct from a more traditional approach to catechetical curriculum.

- First, and most significant, the content is totally discipleship driven. It is almost exclusively defined and shaped by our understanding of the nature of discipleship itself.
- Second, its relevance for those being catechized is derived from their own commitment to be disciples—or at least their openness to explore what discipleship entails. The rationale and validity of the content rests upon the presumption that the catechized have at least this minimum desire to enter more deeply into a relationship with Jesus precisely as his disciples.
- Third, in terms of scope the content is somewhat limited, on the one hand, focusing on what can be considered most fundamental and basic to a life of discipleship—or, as the *GDC* states, "Being essential, it looks to what is 'common' for the Christian, without entering into disputed questions nor transforming itself into a form of theological investigation" (art. 68). On the other hand, it is comprehensive, embracing over time all the basic information, skills, and attitudes required of a disciple.

- Fourth, the content is intended to provide the basis for a true apprenticeship. As such, it presumes the ongoing experiences provided in the "content" of catechesis as encounter and catechesis as initiation. It is not, therefore, ever simply academic or abstract. It is eminently practical, always oriented to helping the catechized learn how to deal with the concrete circumstances and challenges a disciple encounters in the church and society today.
- Fifth, the content of the apprenticeship needs to be understood, developed, and presented in such a way that it takes into full account the principles of the intellectual and psychological readiness of the various age groups that have evolved in recent decades. In the same way it needs to respect the principles of inculturation and adaptation the *GDC* and other recent documents have set forth.

Guided by these principles we now wish to outline in general terms what the content of our catechesis will contain when we approach it as an apprenticeship for disciples.

There are various ways we can describe the characteristic tasks an apprentice disciple needs to learn. Here we have opted for the description offered by the respected scripture scholar Donald Senior. In a series of lectures entitled *Gospel Discipleship,* published by NCR Tapes in 1980, he examines how each of the four evangelists treats discipleship. He concludes that a disciple can best be described as one required continually to "walk with Jesus, learn from Jesus and participate in the mission of Jesus." To this he adds the important point that the disciple pursues all these tasks, not alone, but in companionship with the community of disciples (the church). We present the main elements of the content of a disciple's apprenticeship around those four themes.

## A DISCIPLE IS ONE WHO CONTINUALLY
## WALKS WITH JESUS

Before getting into some of the specifics of this component of the "curriculum," a clarifying comment is necessary. In our popular understanding we usually consider discipleship to be a temporary stage in our development. We sit at the feet of a master until we acquire enough knowledge and skill to go off on our own and begin to function independently. Such, for example, was the case with Jung, who was once a disciple of Freud. Discipleship with Jesus, however, is a permanent condition, not a stage in development. We do not anticipate a time when we will no longer need to walk in his company, when we will be able to go off on our own and function independently of him. In fact, this ongoing companionship with Jesus is essential to all else we are called upon to do as disciples.

That is why the information and skills to be acquired in this component of the apprenticeship can be considered foundational. It is probably obvious that this component is also intimately related to what we seek to provide in our catechesis viewed as encounter. We are involved here in showing our apprentices not just why but how to remain in the company of Jesus in their daily life. We seek to show them how to walk with, stay in contact with, remain in the presence of, or as youth may say, how to hang out with Jesus. We hope to show them how to be *companions* of Jesus with all the intimacy the root meaning of the word implies (namely, "to share bread with"). This can be considered the goal of this component of the "curriculum."

In doing this we face a unique challenge the first disciples did not face. They could literally walk with Jesus and perceive him with their senses. However, we are trying to help people learn how to walk with the risen Lord, who exists in a realm beyond our senses. Discerning his presence and action obviously requires special skills, including some not easily acquired in today's social and cultural environment. These include the following.

*Sacramental Sensitivity*

It is a theological given that the risen Lord is continually present to us. It is also a theological given that we can become aware of his presence and action through revelatory signs that we call, in theological terms, sacraments. Thus, in order to fulfill the disciple's task of *continually walking with the Lord* we need to be able to recognize him present to us through these signs. This requires that apprentice disciples develop what we describe as sacramental sensitivity—that combination of attentiveness or alertness joined with the capacity for discernment that enables us to recognize and respond to Jesus' presence being revealed through these signs.

Developing this sacramental sensitivity is foundational to the life of a disciple. It is one of the most basic skills required and therefore needs to be given priority in our catechetical content. It is the source of a "sixth sense" that enables us recognize and therefore walk with the risen Lord today. Equipped with this sacramental sensitivity the disciple is able to discover Jesus present in such revelatory signs as nature, relationships, the community, the witness of other disciples. This same sensitivity is needed to experience Jesus' presence revealed to us in a special way in scripture and the sacraments. It can also rightly be described as the door to prayer, that special and unique way to companion Jesus we will discuss shortly.

We are not prepared to explore in detail here the specific concepts, methods, and activities to be used in fostering this sacramental sensitivity. Our primary purpose here is to point out the essential nature this foundational skill plays in the life of a disciple and hence the importance to be given to it in developing our catechetical content in the third millennium. We can say this much, however. In the process of nurturing sacramental sensitivity we will need to give attention to the nature of signs and symbols in general and to those special signs effected by the church, namely, the seven official sacraments, their origins and the history of their development, the role each is to play in the life of a disciple, and the skills needed to enter into them.

While our present curriculums do give some attention to the development of sacramental sensitivity, it is seldom approached systematically or treated as the foundational skill it is. More often the skill itself is given a peripheral or even optional place in our overall courses and the specific lessons presented. The major portion of the time is usually devoted to presenting the theology of the seven sacraments. In an authentic catechesis of discipleship the focus will be first on the skill of sacramental sensitivity in general. A catechesis of the specific sacraments will unfold more gradually.

Developing such sacramental sensitivity is a challenge for any age group at any time. It is even more challenging today in a culture caught up in living at a frenetic pace within an environment that constantly bombards us with a multitude of voices all clamoring and competing for our attention and our patronage. Children and youth seem especially vulnerable to the distractions and deceptions contained in this "noise." Thus, it is all the more urgent that we give special importance to the development of this skill and treat it as an essential element in the content of our disciples' apprenticeship.

*Prayer*

Sacramental sensitivity can be described as a kind of spiritual radar enabling us to spot our target, Jesus, on our screen of consciousness. Prayer, in this analogy, is our effort to zoom in on or engage our target. Though not very poetic, the analogy does show the relationship between sacramental sensitivity and the act of praying. Prayer enables us to enter into a conscious relationship of mutual conversation, attentiveness, and of simply being together. Thus, it is ultimately through prayer that the disciple is able to walk with the risen Lord.

Recently I have heard various catechetical theorists as well as catechists "in the trenches" state that if they could teach only one thing in their ministry, it would be how to pray. Perhaps without realizing it they are echoing a fundamental principle contained in the catechesis of discipleship. If, as the *GDC* says, the "definitive aim of catechesis is to put people not only in touch, but also in communion and intimacy, with Jesus Christ" (art. 80, *CT* 5), then, given the nature of prayer, learning to pray is clearly one of the most critical and basic skills the disciple needs to acquire.

Fortunately, we have been experiencing a virtual renaissance of interest in spirituality in general and prayer in particular in recent years. We now have a wealth of material on every aspect of prayer—the history and components of various schools of prayer within the Catholic tradition, as well as the many forms it can take as witnessed in the various cultures and religious traditions found throughout all parts of the world. Granted, teaching people to pray is always challenging, but today we have a certain interest and momentum to build upon, as well as some marvelous resources for doing so.

It is true that our present catechesis does have a tradition of including time for praying together and its traditional curriculum does include periodic lessons on the nature, importance, and methods of prayer. However, prayer too often has been given less attention than has been given to the teaching of various doctrines and moral truths. It is our contention here that in developing the content for a catechesis of discipleship, *teaching people how to pray* needs to be given a much more prominent place in the apprenticeship program.

*Scripture*

Scripture, especially the gospels, has a privileged place as a sign through which we can experience the presence and action of Jesus. As a means through which disciples can walk with Jesus, praying and reflecting upon the scriptures on a regular basis is an invaluable resource. The skills and knowledge required to approach scripture in this way are therefore considered an essential element of the content of a catechesis of discipleship. Fortunately, the teaching of scripture—in terms of its content or story, the history of its development, and the exegetical skills for reading it intelligently—is one area where the current catechetical curriculum is already doing an excellent job. To a large extent this content can and should be transported "as is" into a catechesis of discipleship and included in the development of this part of the apprentice program.

49

## The Eucharist

Intelligent participation in the Eucharist is the means par excellence for continually walking with Jesus. We can experience Jesus in the gathering of the community; in the songs, rituals, and other symbols used in the celebration; in the proclamation of the word; and ultimately, of course, by sharing in the bread and cup of the sacrificial meal. Thus an integral component in the content of the disciple's apprentice program will be to provide the information and skills required to appreciate and participate intelligently in the Eucharist.

While our present curriculums contain much excellent catechesis on the Eucharist—its nature, purpose, origins, and development—it is too often presented in a somewhat abstract way as theological truth and as an end in itself. As such, participation in Eucharist comes across as a pious religious duty and not as the intimately personal and communal event it is intended to be—a special opportunity to encounter Jesus, a special opportunity to walk with Jesus as his disciple. Though we only cite here the importance the Eucharist should play in the formation of the disciple, in reality every aspect of the church's sacramental life and ritual has an important and highly effective role to play in the formation of disciples. The *GDC* underscores this fact when it says:

> Christ is always present in his Church, especially in "liturgical celebrations" (cf. *SC* 7). Communion with Jesus Christ leads to the celebration of his salvific presence in the sacraments, especially in the Eucharist. The Church ardently desires that all the Christian faithful be brought to that full, conscious and active participation which is required by the very nature of the liturgy (cf. *SC* 14) and the dignity of the baptismal priesthood. (art. 85)

Note that the focus of this aspect of the apprentice program is to help budding disciples learn *how* to participate effectively in the Eucharist and other sacraments. The motivation to do so must come from their more fundamental desire and their awareness of the responsibility to find ways to walk with or live in the presence of the risen Lord. As in all other aspects of the apprentice program, the goal here is to help the catechized acquire specific information and skills needed by disciples. It presupposes of the catechized at least some initial desire or openness to be disciples.

*Summary*

It should be clear that there is a close connection and much similarity between catechesis as encounter and the proposed catechetical content of this aspect of an apprentice program. There is an important distinction between the two, however. We can perhaps use the familiar proverb about giving a fish versus teaching to fish to illustrate it. In catechesis as encounter, the role of the catechist is to provide ad hoc opportunities to encounter Jesus—through carefully planned prayer experiences, spontaneous witness, guided reflections on the gospel, and such. Providing such opportunities is akin to "giving a person a fish." In the apprentice program the goal is to "teach a person to fish" by imparting the information and skills that enable disciples to encounter or walk with Jesus on their own initiative long after they complete their apprenticeship. The aim is to equip them with the capacity to recognize and seize upon the myriad opportunities to do so that are present in their daily life.

As stated earlier, we did not intend here to present a thoroughly developed "curriculum" for this part of the disciple's apprenticeship. Rather, we have tried to sketch out in broad terms the themes or topics we need to develop. We do much the same as we turn to the second component of the disciple's apprenticeship, namely, *learning from Jesus.*

## A DISCIPLE IS ONE WHO CONTINUALLY LEARNS FROM JESUS

The goal in this component of the apprentice program is to present in simple terms the fundamental vision and values Jesus taught and embodied during his ministry on earth. The content, therefore, makes up what we can call a disciple's foundational belief system—that basic vision through which the disciple filters his or her ongoing experience of reality and those values used in guiding concrete decisions and behavior. In addition, the apprentice program needs to equip the disciple with both the attitudes and skills required continually to strive to enter more deeply into the meaning of Jesus' vision and values throughout life. Thus, the apprentice program should also gradually provide the disciple with the information and skills required for effectively drawing upon the church's tradition and the ongoing witness of the living community in this pursuit.

It is important to stress that in this apprentice stage of catechesis we are striving to introduce the disciple to what has sometimes been described in our tradition simply as *the Way*. We are concerned here with Jesus' most fundamental message to his disciples, or what the *GDC* described as "what is 'common' for the Christian" (art. 68). Thus in this stage we are certainly concerned with the church's official theological doctrine but not the technical or formal presentation of it. That kind of formal, systematic development of doctrine with its nuances and subtleties more properly belongs in the next stage of catechesis, described by the *GDC* as the "continuous" or "permanent catechesis" to be provided after one completes the formative stage of apprenticeship and is firmly established as a disciple within the community of disciples (art. 51). In this apprenticeship stage, therefore, we need to present our message in a more kerygmatic way. It should rely more directly upon the sermons, sayings, and parables of Jesus and upon the witness of his actions, and less upon the more technical theological formulations of the doctrines that flow from them.

Here we are at the heart of the paradigm shift required if we are to develop an authentic catechesis of discipleship. This new approach is not supported by most of our current curriculums nor the textbook series that embody them. Also, it seems to fly in the face of those who are urging a "return to basics" and to fostering a true "Catholic identity." We are struggling against 450 years of "catechetical gravity" that requires that we present in systematic fashion our complete belief system, the complete body of truths about Jesus, his teachings, and the church—and that we do this within the first eight years of the catechesis of a child! We will say more about how we need to deal with this very real tension and the concern for a lost Catholic identity in a later chapter. Now let us turn instead to a review of the content that needs to be presented within this component of the apprentice program.

## The Vision of Jesus

The vision Jesus taught is framed by three dominant themes.

1. Jesus taught his followers to regard and approach Yahweh, the all-holy and all-powerful God of Abraham, as their Father, their Abba, a doting parent who loves each of his children with infinite tenderness, who is intimately concerned about every aspect of their person and their life, and who continually extends to them his infinite mercy and forgiveness.

2. Jesus taught that all human beings, regardless of gender, race, or socioeconomic status, are indeed God's beloved children. Each possesses an inestimable dignity and has access to the glorious destiny proper to children of God.

3. Jesus taught a message of certain hope that God's kingdom (rule, dominion, reign) of peace and justice, the beginning signs of which we can glimpse in the present, will be established despite the forces of evil that oppose it and despite the present suffering this evil is causing.

We find this vision summarized in the Our Father, often called the Little Gospel. We see the various themes of this vision vividly, even indelibly portrayed in such parables as the prodigal son and in sayings such as "you are worth more than many sparrows" and "the very hairs of your head are numbered." Jesus continually enfleshes and bears witness to this vision by his own expressions of profound intimacy and complete trust in his Father's love—a witness most poignantly and powerfully expressed throughout his trial and cruci-fixion. His resurrection also gives a definitive witness to the hope his disciples are called to embrace. This vision is dramatically evident, too, in what has come to be called his table ministry, a ministry that foreshadows the ultimate expression and sign of this vision, the eucharistic table, itself foreshadows that time promised by Jesus when all God's children will gather to feast together in their Father's kingdom.

Jesus calls upon his disciples to embrace and understand this vision and allow it to form and shape their own identity. To the degree that they acquire the true characteristics or identity as fol-lowers of Jesus (profound love, gratitude, and trust in God-Abba; profound courage, hope, and even joy despite present adversity; the awareness that all human beings are children of God), they will also embrace a clear set of values to guide them in their rela-tionships with one another. Let's examine these values now.

## Values of Jesus

The values Jesus proposes that his disciples use to guide their actions flow from the above vision, especially the awareness that they and all other human beings are our brothers and sisters, the very children of God endowed with the dignity and destiny proper to chil-dren of God. These values can be grouped into four basic principles, the sources of which are found throughout the teachings of Jesus and continually witnessed to by his own treatment of others.

1. The disciples of Jesus are called to love and respect every-one, including (especially) those who do not seem to deserve love and respect, either because of their own actions or because they do not meet society's standards for "respectability."

2. Because all they possess is in fact a gift from their loving Father, the disciples of Jesus are called upon to share all their gifts with whomever might have need of them.

3. Simply stated, the disciples of Jesus are called upon to forgive everyone everything.

4. Finally, the disciples of Jesus are to judge no one except themselves.

Even a casual reading reveals Jesus teaching these principles to his disciples on every page of the gospels, both by his words and by his actions. We find them at the heart of the Beatitudes and the entire Sermon on the Mount. We find them modeled in the way he continually welcomed warmly and respectfully his society's economic, political, and religious outcasts—the powerless, the poor, lepers, publicans, public sinners, women, and children. He forgives his enemies and encourages his disciples to do the same.

*Summary*

We need to make several observations about the nature of this core message we seek to impart in the apprentice program. First, the gospel that Jesus taught is really that simple. It can certainly be articulated differently from the summary we presented. Regardless of the summary statements and metaphors one may choose to use, however, if it authentically captures Jesus' core message it remains very simple. As such it has the ability to cut across all divisions, whether of social classes, culture, age, gender, or education. But simple does not mean shallow or simplistic. Jesus' teaching is the very wisdom of God. It possesses inexhaustible depth. It is the storehouse described by Jesus from which his disciples have continued to bring forth "new things and old" in each new generation for almost two thousand years.

Second, we should view the apprenticeship program as a time devoted primarily to helping the budding disciples understand and embrace these core truths. It is a time for schooling them in these foundational insights that make up the core of a disciple's identity, or if you prefer, the core of an authentic Catholic identity. It is formation in this core identity that in time provides the lens through which the disciple can begin to appreciate and understand the more formal doctrinal teachings the church has developed over the centuries. For example, a disciple formed in this basic understanding of the gospel can begin to appreciate the wisdom of the church's documents on social justice. Those teachings will resonate with the disciple's core identity. To a person lacking that basic formation, these same teachings will tend to fall on deaf ears.

The very riches of our doctrinal tradition can become an obstacle if we attempt to present them too soon or in too much detail in this stage of the disciple's development. Peripheral truths can begin to seem more important than they actually are, for example. Essential truths and moral principles, viewed in isolation from Jesus' fundamental vision, can seem irrelevant or platitudinous.

Third, this kind of formation takes time. As stated before, our continuing temptation has been to rush through this basic formation in the gospel and turn our attention to presenting more formal (and sometimes peripheral) doctrine. We need to remember and appreciate just how difficult it is (and continues to be throughout life) truly to accept the idea that "God loves me"—infinitely, unconditionally, faithfully. Yet it is only to the degree that we do accept this good news of Jesus that the other dimensions of his teaching begin to make sense. In the same way, we need to remember and appreciate how radical a conversion is entailed before we can begin consistently to respect or love everyone, forgive everyone, share all our gifts—especially with those whom society deems undeserving of our love, our forgiveness, our generosity. Hence, we need to revisit these most basic truths over and over throughout the apprenticeship, using all the creativity and imagination at our command to find ways to make them fresh and appealing for each age group and at each stage in the individual disciple's development.

Fourth, the message of Jesus remains quite radical even after two thousand years. It still flies in the face of and threatens the conventional wisdom and values that shape many of the political, economic, social, and even religious institutions today, just as it did in Jesus' time. If we shape our behavior according to the teaching of

Jesus, we will often be judged immoral, irreverent, unpatriotic, or even criminal today, just as Jesus and the first disciples were judged in their time.

Fifth, the logic or validity of Jesus' values is rooted in his vision of reality. There is obviously an intimate connection between the vision he teaches and the way of life he calls his disciples to adopt. If we accept that God is a loving, merciful parent, if we accept the dignity all human beings possess as children of God and the familial bond this creates among us, if we accept the reality and certainty of our ability to overcome evil and death, then the behavior outlined in his values makes preeminent sense. Therefore, to be effective in our catechesis we must be careful that we present and demonstrate this unity that exists between Jesus' vision and the behavior he expects of his disciples. The vision is necessary to motivate and fuel the behavior or good works. The good works, in turn, bear witness to the reality of the vision and serve to incarnate it in time and space.

This mention of witness provides a natural transition to the next theme in the content of the apprentice program, namely, learning how to participate in the mission of Jesus.

## A DISCIPLE CONTINUALLY PARTICIPATES IN THE MISSION OF JESUS

The gospels make it quite clear that Jesus gathered disciples around him and patiently trained them so they could continue to carry out his mission after he was gone. He took special pains to ensure that they understood his teachings. He formed them into a community for their mutual support. He taught them to pray and to rely on prayer. He sent them out on "practice" missions. Today's disciples have the same responsibility to participate in the mission of Jesus, and their apprenticeship of necessity must involve providing them with similar understandings and skills so they can enter effectively into that same mission.

The first step in developing such apprentice training is to clarify the precise nature of Jesus' mission, since it is that mission into which we hope to introduce the apprentice disciples. As the scriptures state, Jesus came to bear witness to the good news of the reality and certainty of the coming of God's reign. He was also sent to be the instrument through which God overcomes once and for all the forces of evil that oppose its establishment. Integral to that good news is Jesus' witness to God's infinite, all-merciful and ever-faithful love for humanity and to the dignity each human possesses precisely as a child of God.

This aspect of the disciple's training, then, has two dimensions. Disciples have to be trained to be witnesses; they are to understand what it means to be instruments. Let us first examine the nature of witness.

### Training to Be Witnesses

Jesus bore witness to the reality of God's love, God's reign, and our human dignity both by his words (his proclamation and teaching) and by his actions—how he related to whomever he encountered, whether the rich and powerful or the poor, the oppressed, the sick and afflicted. He called upon his disciples to do the same—to make the reality of the good news present to others both by their words and by their deeds.

Jesus not only taught *what* his disciples are to witness to but also *how* they are to go about it. In his own efforts to witness to the good news Jesus never resorted to coercion, violence, or similar tactics of power, force, and manipulation that society's institutions often use to get others to conform to their views. In training his disciples he made it clear they too must avoid such tactics at all costs. He told them they are to be for others what *salt* is to food, what *light* is to a darkened room, what *yeast* is to a mound of dough. Salt does not control food; it preserves it and brings out its best qualities. Light does not change a room; it enables those in it to see clearly and move about freely. Yeast does not shape dough to its likeness; it enables the dough to achieve its own true potential.

In training his disciples to be witnesses Jesus also stressed their need for each other. He sent them out in pairs. He formed them into a community where they could derive mutual support, mutual instruction, and the courage they would need to confront resistance and persecution. In this regard Jesus was quite frank in warning them that they would indeed meet opposition and persecution in their efforts to witness to the good news.

## Instruments

This aspect of preparing disciples for their mission is much more difficult on two levels. It is more difficult to grasp and more challenging to carry out. It is in this aspect of the mission that we need to deal with the role the cross must play in the disciple's life. Jesus was quite explicit in this regard. He told his disciples in no uncertain terms that, like him, they too must pick up the cross.

To understand what this means we have to recall two basic theological principles in our tradition. First, it is God alone who is establishing the reign of God. We can do nothing to bring it about by our own efforts. Second, it is through God's power alone that the forces of evil, which continue to attempt to resist and impede the coming of God's reign, ultimately will be overcome.

In light of these two principles we can draw two important conclusions in terms of the nature of the disciple's mission. First, in our efforts to participate in the mission of Jesus we are to consider ourselves *instruments* of God, totally dependent upon God for success. As scriptures state, some of us may be instruments for sowing, others instruments for reaping, but in final analysis God is the One who actually causes the increase.

Second, to be an effective instrument requires that we put ourselves totally at God's disposal. We must sacrifice ourselves to God. The root meaning of sacrifice (from the Latin *sacer,* "sacred," and *facere,* "to make") is precisely that. We make something sacred when we it aside solely for God's use or put it totally at the disposal of the God. How do we as human beings possessing free will sacrifice ourselves, put ourselves totally at God's disposal, transform ourselves into authentic instruments for God's use? Through obedience.

Because the ancients often used physical immolation as a way to sacrifice or put something totally at God's disposal, sacrifice in popular piety now tends to be associated almost exclusively with physical pain or deprivation. For many people, the cross, which we know and celebrate as the sacrifice par excellence, tends to reinforce that concept. In reality, however, the sacrificial cross Jesus requires his disciples to pick up is the same one he carried, namely, the act of putting oneself totally at God's disposal through obedience. It was Jesus' obedience—even unto death on the cross—that transformed him into the instrument God used to conquer the forces of evil and the power of death. The degree of his suffering was not important in some quantitative sense. Many others have actually suffered much greater pain for a much longer time in their journey to death. Rather, the intensity of his suffering serves primarily to illustrate the total and unwavering quality of his trust in and obedience to his Father.

It is in this light that we need to present the cross in our apprentice program. It is as an integral part of participating in the mission of Jesus. But what disciples need to realize is that their success as effective instruments for promoting God's reign depends on the degree to which they are able to continue to trust in God and put themselves at God's disposal. We do not train disciples to seek pain, suffering, hardship, or deprivation. Rather, we train them to be able to continue to trust in and obey God in all circumstances, *including* those that involve pain, suffering, hardship, or deprivation. That is the core message contained in the example of Jesus' own cross and what Jesus is asking of his disciples when calling upon them to take up their cross.

In this context we need to help disciples understand that success in ministry is to be measured in terms of the degree to which we are able to hold ourselves and our initiatives at God's disposal. It is true that we need to dedicate ourselves to our mission with all the intelligence, talent, and creativity we possess. But success should not measured by the number of goals we are able to achieve. Rather, we need to remember that God can and will utilize even our apparent failures, mistakes, and shortcomings on behalf of the kingdom provided we maintain this attitude of trust and obedience. In terms of human logic, for example, Jesus was a complete failure. Despite his total dedication to his mission, only a small handful of people remained loyal to him at his death. Yet because of Jesus' unwavering trust and obedience, we know God was able to transform that apparent failure into the very foundation stone upon which the kingdom is built. It will be the same for us when we participate in the mission of Jesus as disciples.

This is not the place to explore all the implications and nuances of what the scriptures and tradition tell us about what it means to be a witness to the good news and an instrument for building the kingdom. Nor can we outline in detail the precise nature of the "curriculum" of information and skills we need to impart at each stage in the apprentice program. The only point we wish to stress here is that a catechesis of discipleship will contain such a "curriculum" for imparting the skills and information required to be an effective witness and instrument in today's society. And like Jesus' own training program, it should include ongoing opportunities for practice.

## A DISCIPLE CONTINUALLY PARTICIPATES IN THE LIFE OF THE COMMUNITY OF DISCIPLES, THE CHURCH

It is the task of catechesis viewed as initiation to introduce budding disciples into the fullness of the life of community in all its facets: its creed and tradition, its symbols and ritual celebrations, and the variety of ministries its mission embraces. In terms of apprenticeship the task will be more generic (or humanistic), namely, to foster in the catechized those foundational skills and attitudes required for participation in any group or community. We have in mind here such things as helping everyone develop and maintain an attitude of basic respect for each person in the group; the ability and willingness to be truly attentive to and respectful of what others say, their ideas, values, and convictions; the ability and willingness to be sensitive as well to their unspoken feelings, needs, hurts, and concerns.

This aspect of the apprentice program would also include gradually fostering the basic skills required for dialogue, consensus building, group decision-making, conflict resolution, and problem solving. It will involve nurturing a sense of responsibility for the well-being of the group and the ability to recognize when it is necessary to set aside one's personal interests to attain a common good. It will involve helping individuals recognize and appreciate the unique gifts and talents they have to contribute to the group as well as the importance of recognizing and affirming the gifts of others.

Some of these goals can and should lend themselves to periodic formal instruction (for example, the rules for good listening, and processes that can be used in group problem solving). At the same time, much of what we would hope to impart in this dimension of the apprentice program can and should be taught by the very way we structure our program and the modeling and example we provide when are conducting it. Even if some of our children and youth are being exposed to many of these same skills and attitudes in their formal education programs and social organizations (such as Scouts), we need to take special pains to promote them through their catechesis as well in order to help them realize these skills and attitudes have a very important role to play in being good members of the community of disciples as well.

## CONCLUSION

As can be seen, the above outline of the content for a catechesis of discipleship includes virtually all the topics found in our existing catechetical curriculum—sacraments, scripture, prayer, morality, and the church. However, it should be equally obvious that we will approach many of those topics quite differently. When the focus of our catechesis is discipleship, and it is carried out within the framework of an apprenticeship, we do effect a kind of paradigm shift.

First, the emphasis any particular topic receives is determined by the importance of its role in the life of a disciple. Foundational insights and skills of discipleship take precedence. For example, learning to pray has a central rather than a peripheral position in the content. Second, most topics take on concreteness, relevance, and practical value in the immediate life of the disciple. They are oriented to *being* a disciple rather than to *learning about* the faith. Third, the treatment of each topic is more kerygmatic than theological or academic. Finally, as we will see in the next chapter, we need to adapt much of our current methodology and our program structures in order to present this content effectively. We turn now to that task.

# 4

# A Shift in Structures: Part One

## INTRODUCTION

The *GDC* states: "The concept of catechesis which one has, profoundly conditions the selection and organization of its content *(cognitive, experiential, behavioral)*, identifies those to whom it is addressed and *defines the pedagogy to be employed in accomplishing its objectives*" (art. 35, final emphasis added). We saw in the last chapter how our understanding of content changes radically when catechesis is understood as formation in discipleship. We now want to see how this same understanding of catechesis affects our pedagogy—the structures and methods to be employed in accomplishing our objective.

Just as the goal helps determine the most effective way to structure our program, so the program structures we adopt will tend to dictate which methods are most appropriate and effective. Let us begin by considering how best to structure our catechesis of discipleship. This will be a somewhat theoretical analysis. In the following chapter we examine some of the practical issues involved in implementing the proposed model. Then in chapter 6 we examine the implications this has on our methodology.

At the core of the catechesis of discipleship is relationship—relationship both with Jesus and with the other disciples of Jesus or the community. The experience of history and more recent scientific evidence of modern psychology testify to the fact that relationships of any kind are most effectively fostered in what we commonly call the small-group setting. It seems logical, then, to assume that the most effective way to structure our catechesis of discipleship is to take the lead provided by the RCIA and move it from an essentially academic or classroom model to a more relational or small-group model.

This is no new concept. For over a generation innovative catechists have been attempting to develop alternative models for doing catechesis to replace the academic model of catechesis we inherited almost five hundred years ago. The reason so many of these alternative models have failed to take root, despite the imagination and creativity employed in developing them, is becoming clear. Consciously or unconsciously, most people who have developed and initiated various alternative models never sufficiently changed their understanding of the goal of catechesis; they still sought to achieve the same catechetical goals the academic model was designed to achieve. Though they may have often used the rhetoric of discipleship in speaking of their goals, the understandings and aspirations of our more traditional catechesis still seemed to maintain power over them. Truly alternative models require that we formulate a truly alternative goal. This may become clearer if we compare some of the structural implications of the academic versus the relational or small-group model.

## ACADEMIC AND RELATIONAL MODELS— SOME COMPARISONS

In terms of *physical setting,* the academic model suggests some form of classroom context or atmosphere—no matter how creatively the seating is arranged or how cheerfully it is appointed. Furniture and equipment are selected with an eye to the imparting and mastery of information. For example, desks or tables to facilitate writing are chosen over sofas or easy chairs. The intention is to create something of a laboratory (from *labor,* "work") or task-oriented atmosphere. All of this is appropriate when the goal is an academic one. But when the goal is more relational, such a classroom setting is actually detrimental.

In terms of *scheduling,* the academic model requires a certain rigor and continuity. Topics need to unfold and be presented in orderly fashion. Missing a lesson can be very disruptive for an individual, and it also complicates the teacher's task because of needed "make-up work." Holidays and unplanned interruptions in the schedule (such as a snow day) can have a similar disruptive effect. The logical presentation of the material requires this kind of regular scheduling as well as the need to cover the assigned curriculum by a given time. This is as it should be when the goal is academic. But if the goal is relational, the schedule can be much more flexible, occasional absences by individuals are far less detrimental to their overall growth, and holidays can become occasions for gathering rather than disruptions in a schedule.

In terms of *grouping*, the academic model tends to place students into grades by chronological age—one grade for each age group. The grades may or not be further subdivided according to the students' abilities to achieve the academic goals for that grade level. In the relational model there is much more flexibility. Chronological age and even academic ability do not play such critical roles. The focus is more on relational skills and needs. Children at ages seven and nine have much in common, for example, as do children between the ages of eleven and fourteen. Thus it is possible to form groups within certain ranges of chronological age. Also, it is possible at times to employ intergenerational groups very effectively in the relational model.

In the academic model the *teacher-student relationship* tends to be defined by the classical principles of pedagogy: the teacher establishes the goals, determines how the students will reach them, and evaluates their success. We have moved far beyond the concept of the teacher with a menacing hickory stick in hand ruling over passive students. Today's teachers seek to create an atmosphere that encourages students to become actively involved, question, explore, and experiment. But the teacher remains the "expert" who sets the goals and determines how they are to be reached. In the relational model the leader is viewed much more as a facilitator or as a more experienced mentor who is also a participant in the learning process, a co-learner. In the relational model, everyone's experience is valued. The role of "expert" can move from person to person depending on circumstances. There is also much more freedom to deviate from preestablished goals and move in some other direction, guided by the spirit (Spirit) of the moment. Success, evaluated by the group itself, is measured in terms of nurturing, deepening, or healing relationships more than successfully covering a certain amount of material in the curriculum.

All of these examples support a basic contention in this work; that is, the academic model continues to drive the majority of our catechesis despite all our efforts at renewal. It seems to be embedded in our very bones. We continue to talk of and schedule teacher training sessions for our catechists. Our program is developed as a series of lessons supported by lesson plans that flow from a formal curriculum contained in formal textbooks. Our programs tend to revolve around society's academic year and are communicated to parents in the form of a class schedule. Children are grouped into grades by chronological age, typically meet in formal classrooms or in spaces we try to set up as makeshift classrooms. All this makes sense, of course, as long as we consciously or unconsciously view the goal of catechesis in academic terms, that is, as a body of truths to be imparted. Our instincts will continue to draw us back to this model until we succeed in breaking once and for all from such an understanding of catechesis and reclaim discipleship as the rightful goal of catechesis.

Again we must make it clear that we are not promoting the catechesis of discipleship as if it were some contentless, "feel good" endeavor. An authentic catechesis of discipleship supports the need to learn the various truths contained in our creed and our tradition. It involves a certain orderliness or discipline—the very meaning of which is derived from the word *disciple.* But we continue to maintain that the learning of these truths has to be approached within the context of discipleship. We have to present these truths as rooted in and flowing from one's relationship with Jesus—as ways better to articulate, understand, and live out that relationship. Presented apart from or in the absence of that relationship, they tend to be uninspiring, irrelevant, or quaint at best, and incomprehensible at worst.

Hence, we continue to maintain that the truths of our faith are best introduced and explained within the context of forming a relationship with Jesus. If we make the nurturing of that relationship our goal and structure our catechesis accordingly, we will in the very process also have ample opportunity effectively to teach the truths of the faith needed by disciples of Jesus. Let us now examine in more detail the nature and implications of the relational or small-group model for structuring our catechesis.

## HOW THE SMALL-GROUP MODEL WORKS

Perhaps the best way to identify and illustrate the components involved in structuring our catechesis along the lines of the relational or small-group model is with a concrete example. A few years ago a pastoral minister/DRE in our parish invited a group of men to explore the possibilities of forming a prayer group. Over two months the following format evolved quite naturally.

- A group of men ranging in age from the early thirties to the early sixties gather every Thursday morning at the parish center a little before 6:30 in the morning. Attendance any given week varies from a low of five to a high of fifteen but consistently averages around eight to ten.
- The first fifteen minutes or so are spent in the kitchen having a cup of coffee and waiting for the stragglers. This time is filled initially with lively greetings, some friendly banter, and chatting about last week's game or some current headline. The talk moves quite naturally to more personal sharing of the successes and crises, the blessings and trials one or another has experienced at home or at work during the past week. The group listens attentively as a member recounts the progress a sick child is making or a frustration encountered in tending to an aging parent. Totally unstructured and unplanned, this has become an integral

part of the overall experience, a period of bonding, of giving and receiving heartfelt support.

- As if on cue someone will say, "I guess we ought to get started," and the group moves upstairs, coffee cups in hand, to a pleasant room furnished with comfortable chairs and sofas arranged roughly in a circle. Spontaneously, three individuals volunteer to read each of the next Sunday's readings from a lector's booklet. There are different volunteers each week. The others follow the readings in their own booklets. After the readings there is a quiet period for personal reflection. Some weeks it is as short as three or four minutes before someone speaks up. Other weeks the personal reflection can last up to ten minutes before the silence is broken.

- Next follows a time of sharing, loosely structured around each man's personal response to several basic questions: What words, phrases, or images seemed to "leap out" at you? What do you think God might be saying to you (us) in one or another of these readings? What do you think we might we say or do in response?

   The majority of the men in this group are far from experts in theology. Yet each week I continue to be truly edified and often awed by the wisdom that emerges during this sharing. The men listen with attention and sincere respect to whoever is sharing. Alternative views are often offered. These are intended and received as just that, other ways to look at something based on one's personal experience. The group seems instinctively to avoid rebutting another's view. There is no posturing, no attempts at one-upmanship. The DRE or I is sometimes asked to clarify a scriptural reference or to state "what the church teaches" about some point. But neither of us is looked upon as a teacher or facilitator by the group. We are equal participants who have some expertise in certain areas. Others are regarded as experts in other areas in keeping with their professions and experience.

- There is no predetermined goal or purpose for the gatherings. Other than the scriptures themselves, there is no set content or agenda. There is no formal facilitator. At times the group drifts away from the topic at hand, but inevitably someone brings it back into focus with an appropriate comment or observation. People do not take turns or follow any particular order in sharing. The sharing just happens.
- The group espouses no particular cause and is not consciously action oriented, but in the context of the sharing many practical implications do emerge for dealing with issues or problems at work or in the family from the gospel's perspective. Lives are being changed. For example, one young bachelor member recently decided to use his vacation time to do volunteer work at a mission clinic in Haiti. Many less dramatic but equally edifying commitments to live out gospel values—at home, in the work place, within the parish—have been generated through these shared reflections.
- Near the end of the time together the group gathers in a circle and spends a few minutes offering spontaneous prayers of petition, gratitude, and such, and the session ends with the doxology.

We are not suggesting this as a model to be duplicated in structuring our catechesis. For example, it possesses certain characteristics as an adult group we shouldn't expect to find with a group of twelve year olds. However, it does illustrate certain relational or small-group principles we can use effectively in structuring our catechesis. Let us take a look at these.

## BASIC PRINCIPLES OF THE SMALL-GROUP MODEL

*Invitation to Participate*

When the goal is academic and the academic model is employed, attendance in a catechetical program is more or less mandatory, based on the principle that we have something the students need and they had better attend or else. When the goal is discipleship and the small-group or relational model is used, attendance is more invitational and volitional, based on the principle that each participant is valued as a person, that each has something to give the group, and that each person's gifts are needed by the group, and that a person's participation is truly valued by the group.

Granted, applying this principle of invitation is much more of a challenge when we are dealing with children and youth than when we are dealing with adults. Yet it remains a foundational principle if we become serious in our attempt to shift the structure of our catechesis from the academic to a more relational model. It requires us to reexamine how we take that most fundamental and necessary step of "getting the kids into the program." It suggests, for example, that the traditional "Sign Up Sunday," which puts the burden on parents and is rooted in the underlying presumption of mandatory attendance, might be inappropriate. It forces us to ask questions:

- How can we extend a personal invitation to each youth? Who should do the inviting? Is it appropriate to involve peers in inviting peers? What is the proper role of parents in the process?
- How can we communicate to those invited that we sincerely value their gifts and need their participation (as opposed to a reminding them that they are *expected* to attend a certain number of classes)?
- How can we frame the invitation to ensure that it ultimately comes across as an invitation from Jesus, that it is an invitation to discipleship with him?
- How do we adapt the nature of the invitation and processes for extending it to different age groups so that it takes into account their capacities and limits to hear and respond to it?

I have no ready or facile answers to offer to these and similar questions that arise if we attempt to apply this principle of invitation in structuring our catechetical program. Yet I have no doubt

71

that the catechetical community has the creativity and resources to answer them if we choose to adopt such a principle as a part of our catechetical agenda for the third millennium. In any event, the principle of invitation remains the critical first step in such a shift.

*Community Building or Interpersonal Bonding*

Most serious attempts at renewal in catechesis during the past forty years have acknowledged and attempted to integrate community building into their programming and processes. However, because most of the "new" catechesis has continued to take place within the more restrictive framework of the academic model, these efforts usually have borne little fruit. Too often efforts at community building have gradually been reduced to certain icebreakers and other optional activities in the "lesson plan."

Psychology and the social sciences make it clear that the personal bonding that lies at the heart of any authentic community or support group tends to develop informally when members have time to get to know one another. These disciplines also point out that such bonding in most instances is a slow, gradual process through which the participants begin to drop their defenses and become more secure, trusting, and comfortable in one another's company. Thus, in the beginning stages of community or group development, it is usually necessary to devote considerable time to creating a safe setting and providing opportunities for informal sharing of personal stories, interests, aspirations, and concerns.

Applying these principles to the task of restructuring our catechesis according to a small-group or relational model involves a shift in our thinking. Conditioned by the academic model, which is to a large extent product oriented, we have been trained to use our time efficiently. Chatting over coffee would hardly be an efficient use of time if the above cited group's goal was to learn about prayer, for example. But if the underlying goal is growth in discipleship through shared prayer, then any time spent in informal sharing, in getting to know one another better at the personal level, and in expressing concern over problems encountered is invaluable. In the context of changing our catechetical structures this means we must become willing to direct much more of our energy and much more of our "catechetical time" to fostering personal bonding within the group, especially in the beginning stages of the group's life. Such a commitment will seem less drastic or irresponsible to the degree that we can cease being driven by the more immediate goals of some "curriculum" and instead embrace the idea that we are involved in a more gradual and long-term goal of discipleship formation.

In this same context we can begin to appreciate that "catechetical time" is not confined to a fifty-minute lesson in a classroom. Any place and any time the group gathers has the potential to be very valuable "catechetical time." Though it can be simply stated, the change required in how we view time—especially given its seeming scarcity and the consequent value we place on it in today's society—is one of the most radical and challenging "conversions" involved in effecting the desired paradigm shift to the relational model.

We maintain, then, that the development of this sense of bonding or of community is foundational to the relational model and therefore needs to be given much greater priority in our structuring of our catechetical programs and the use of our time together. Several other important implications also flow from this principle.

- We need to reconsider the *optimum size* of the groupings we form for catechetical purposes. Twenty students may be an optimum size when employing the academic model. Eight to twelve persons tends to be the optimum if we hope to form a relational group. The logistics of structuring the catechetical program along those lines at first glance will seem overwhelming for any large parish involving hundreds of young people. Even smaller parishes, because of more limited resources of personnel and space, will tend to be daunted by the prospect. Such a reaction is totally understandable and justified when one continues to think in terms of an academic model. But, as

73

we hope to show in the next chapter, many of the anticipated problems actually do not materialize if we fully
grasp the true nature of the small-group or relational
model and the resources needed to implement it.

- A second implication flowing from the principle of bonding is the *need for continuity*. We tend in the academic
model to dissolve classes at the end of the academic year
and form new ones the next year. The fact that next year's
class usually contains a mix of new and veteran members
is not a problem. However, in the relational model this is a
serious problem. It can take a half year or longer before a
group begins to feel any true sense of being a community
or developing the basic characteristics of an authentic support group. In the relational model it is foolhardy to dissolve such a group once it has formed, based solely on
some arbitrary calendar date, and then to attempt to form
all new groups on another equally arbitrary date. In the
relational model we will have to be committed to attempting to sustain the continuity and hence the life of our catechetical groups over several years or longer. Ideally, the
same facilitator would remain with the group over that
period. At the minimum we must avoid dissolving such
groups arbitrarily for the convenience of the schedule.

- *Frequency of meetings* is another matter we need to consider if we are serious about structuring our catechesis with
an eye to fostering interpersonal bonds within the group.
The adult group mentioned above meets throughout the
year. It does not restrict itself by an arbitrary academic calendar. Granted, attendance varies at some times in the year.
Individuals may "miss" several weeks in a row when they
go off on a family vacation or a business trip. But the group
continues to meet. Those who are absent are missed, but
they are not "missing something," as would be the case if
the group were following some rigid curriculum. In fact, on
their return they usually enrich the group by sharing their

74

experiences. Implied here, of course, is the move to year-round catechesis. We can expect the resistance to such a concept to be tremendous—among parents, youth, and the catechetical community itself—so deeply is our present catechesis tied to an academic model and consequently an academic year. Virtually all the seemingly legitimate objections raised by these groups will lose their legitimacy, however, if we can begin to understand catechesis in more relational terms as discipleship formation. Only when the goal of catechesis ceases to be academic do we become truly free to consider alternative ways to structure our program. Then we begin to see the value and validity of meeting throughout the year in small support groups.

The shift from an academic to a relational model demands a totally new approach to gathering people together. It calls for a radical shift in the priority we give to the time needed to form interpersonal or community bonds, the length of time a group stays together, and the frequency with which it meets. It demands an equally radical shift in the way we approach the question of how we deal with the content of our catechesis, as we will see next.

## Content

Several issues are involved here, and we will treat each in turn: selection of content, resources to be used, and general method of presentation.

### SELECTION OF CONTENT

The overarching principle here is that whatever the topic with which the group deals, it can somehow be related to the skills and attitudes needed by a disciple (as outlined in the previous chapter). The group's focus will be to develop one or other of those skills and attitudes involved in walking with, learning from, and participating in the mission of Jesus, and doing so as members of a community of disciples.

We must beg the question here insofar as such an apprentice program is yet to be developed in any systematic sense. As indicated in the previous chapter, that task is one of the crucial items in the catechetical agenda for the third millennium. We are not prepared to say, for example, at what point and to what age group we introduce a particular skill, such as how to read scripture intelligently. But whenever that topic is introduced, it will be presented as an essential skill that enables us to continue to walk with Jesus, not as an abstract academic requirement in an academic curriculum.

RESOURCES

The proper resource will be determined by the topic. The actual availability of resources is in one sense virtually unlimited. We have the word of God, of course. There is the witness we get from the countless stories of the heroes of our tradition, as well as the witness of contemporary heroes. In due time, when we have succeeded in formulating in a more systematic way the content of the apprentice program, no doubt the catechetical community with its creativity will begin to develop a variety of "apprentice handbooks" for the various age groups to replace our existing textbooks. These will serve as invaluable resources in much the same way as textbooks have served the academic model of catechesis. As we do now, we can draw on films and videos, contemporary music, events, poetry, and fiction. In short, the availability of resources for presenting content is limited only by our imagination, provided the focus remains that of learning to be disciples.

PRESENTATION OF CONTENT

We are not concerned here with the mechanics or methodology for presenting the chosen resource. We say more about that in another chapter. Rather, we are concerned here with the overall spirit and rationale that should shape the presentation of content.

*Presentation should always be treated as an invitation to prayerful reflection.* Whatever is presented needs to treated in the context of our prayerful and ongoing search for the answer to this basic question: What must I do to grow in my relationship to Jesus?

Stated differently, all material needs to be presented with the intention and in a manner that helps us ask these questions: What might God be calling me to be, to become, to let go of, or to embrace as a disciple of Jesus? What might this scripture passage, this story of a person's deeds or misdeeds, this creedal statement of our tradition, this account of this recent event, or the lyrics of this song be revealing to me in this regard? What good does it reveal for me to pursue as a disciple of Jesus or what evil does it uncover that I must reject?

The idea of prayerful reflection is certainly not new to catechesis. Our current catechetical programs often offer opportunities for prayerful reflection of the kind described above. But when introduced in a more academic context such reflection is frequently treated as an optional activity within the lesson plan rather than integral to it. In the small-group or relational approach we are recommending, prayerful reflection *is* the lesson plan in a sense, framing and providing the mindset for dealing with whatever is presented during the entire time together.

Critical to this approach is the need to allow sufficient time for quiet, personal reflection after the content is presented. The time needed will vary depending on the nature of the content and how it is presented (for example, reading a scripture passage is different from viewing a video) and the age of the group. For example, older children and youth can spend more time in personal reflection than small children. This quiet time will be viewed as both normal and necessary by the participants once we succeed in establishing the attitude of prayerful reflection as the accepted ambiance for the group's time together.

*Processing Content*

There is no mystery here. The process is simply to respect the well-documented principles, dynamics, and ground rules for effective small-group sharing. Everyone's view has value and is to be respected. Everyone needs to develop good listening skills. No one person is to dominate the conversation. Anything even approaching personal ridicule, hurtful comments, or put-downs is out of bounds. As much as possible, decisions are made by consensus. Participants need to develop sensitivity so they can be attentive to the feelings as well as the ideas of others. Members are free to remain silent on a subject if they choose. Rules of common courtesy—such as Don't interrupt another—apply.

The younger and less experienced the group members, the more active the catechist/facilitator's role will be on several levels: formulating questions or providing activities designed to initiate and stimulate sharing (for example, a problem-solving activity); guiding the sharing so that it stays within the general boundaries of the topic at hand; explaining the "rules" for sharing and helping the group "enforce" them if they should be ignored. The more mature the age group and the longer the participants spend time together as a group, the less they will depend upon the facilitator to function and share effectively.

The specific content or topic around which sharing takes place in any given session should be related to some goal in the overall apprentice program (for example, a prayer skill, some aspect of the vision of Jesus, a challenge connected with participating in the mission of Jesus). However, as is the nature of authentic group sharing, there is no way to predict how that topic will unfold, what will come to be viewed as most important by the group, what practical implications group members may arrive at for their own lives. There will be a certain open-endedness in this approach, and often the results exceed what was initially hoped for by the catechist/facilitator. So while the catechist/facilitator does have a definite role to play and may justifiably have a set of goals in mind, a kind of "hidden agenda" of particular insights, principles, or practices he or she hopes the group arrives at, these may have to await discovery on another day.

Since the process is not restricted by the academic model's demand that a certain amount of the curriculum's material be mastered within a certain length of time, it is much easier to adapt to unplanned excursions in other directions. The process of discipleship formation is by its nature more gradual, less easily regimented. It is more psychological than logical. It is more existential and personal and thereby more open to and dependent on the Spirit's influences. The catechist can afford to be patient and need not feel the urgency to accomplish certain goals "on schedule," as is required in the academic model.

### Application to Life

In the academic model much of what is learned does not lend itself to an immediate application to the student's life. It is information to be stored away for later use. In the context of discipleship formation virtually everything presented has a certain pragmatic purpose. It is aimed at affecting in the present one's relationship and consequent behavior precisely as a disciple of Jesus.

Thus, in the model we are proposing the group sharing flows quite naturally and almost inevitably toward practical implications—a skill to be developed, an attitude to be adopted, a new way of behaving or relating to be initiated. The discovery of these implications sometimes requires the help and prompting of the catechist. Just as often the participants arrive at them on their own. In either case, because they have their roots in what has been reflected upon together and is experienced as the more or less logical consequences of that sharing, they do not appear arbitrary or artificial. As stated, the catechist's role will often involve helping the participants articulate these implications in more concrete terms and challenging them to follow through with specific resolves. Yet the motivation and rationale for actually carrying out these implications, once discovered, are integral to the overall purpose and process of discipleship formation.

### Closure

Finally, the typical small-group session ends with some act of closure. If the whole session takes place in the context of a prayerful reflection, this closure serves as a kind of group "Amen" to the session. This "Amen" may take the form of some simple ritual that the group employs regularly. It may vary with each session, taking its form from the nature of the topic for that session. In either case it need not be elaborate. It will usually involve the following elements: participants thank God and petition for God's continuing support; they pledge to carry the fruit of their sharing into their lives in some concrete form; they affirm each other; and they send one another forth with the "kiss of peace" and the promise to gather again soon.

The desired effect of this "Amen" is to affirm what was experienced in the session and to claim personal ownership of it. It is intended to give value and validity to that particular session. In short, it is saying the time together was not "just another class" ended by the ringing of a bell. Rather, the "Amen" is saying it was an "important moment," a time of grace in the journey to mature discipleship.

### The Catechist's Role

As observed several times already, the catechist's role in the small-group or relational model we are proposing is that of facilitator, not teacher. Once we are able to let go of the academic model for catechesis, there are implications for how we recruit and train catechists as well as for the expectations we have for them. This shift from teacher to facilitator can give us a totally new approach to how we address certain perennial "catechist" problems.

## CONCLUSION

We can summarize the basic components of the relational or small-group structure we are proposing as follows:

- Participants' involvement is rooted in a sense of being invited rather than mandated.

- High priority and adequate time are given to helping participants develop the characteristics of a community or support group: mutual respect, mutual trust, mutual concern for one another's well-being, and an overall group identity.

- Participants are grouped by psychological affinity rather than chronological age or academic class year. Groups are kept small, gather regularly throughout the year, and maintain continuity over a span of several years whenever possible.

- The overall ambiance is one of prayerful reflection.

- Content for reflection is chosen because of its relevance for acquiring a particular skill or attitude of discipleship, is reflected upon through the process of group sharing, and is applied to life through that sharing.

- Each session ends with some form of closure or "Amen."

- The catechist's role is that of facilitator.

As the summary shows, the concept and components of the relational or small-group model are hardly revolutionary to anyone familiar with the development of catechesis over the past forty years. Catechetical programs built around this model were introduced and experimented with in the late 1960s and throughout the 1970s. The RCIA, introduced in 1971 and declared normative for catechesis, employs many of the principles of the relational model in its structure. We find many of these same principles present in the workings of the ecclesial base communities that have come to play such a large part in the revitalization of the church in various countries in Latin America. The RENEW program, which has been used quite effectively in many dioceses throughout the United States, is built around many of these same principles. One can even argue that the concept is as old as the church itself and was the "model" employed by Jesus in the very first apprentice program for disciples.

It is safe to say that most challenges to a proposal that we adopt the small-group or relational model as the preferred structure for doing catechesis in the third millennium will not be based on the validity of the concept as such. Rather, challenges will tend to focus on the practical problems one can anticipate in attempting to implement such a structure in any wide-scale manner. The actual implementation of this proposed shift in the way we structure our catechetical programs does indeed raise a number of very practical problems and questions. We examine some of them next.

# 5

# A Shift in Structures: Part Two

## INTRODUCTION

For over a decade the catechetical community has been wrestling with several concerns or problems that impede our efforts to carry out the ministry. First, there is the issue of numbers. In many urban and suburban areas throughout the country the general growth in the Catholic population is resulting in an ever-increasing number of children and youth eligible for catechesis. At the same time it is becoming more difficult each year to find a sufficient number of adults willing to serve as catechists, both at the professional or full-time level and as volunteers. There is often a lack of adequate space and funds to cover the growing costs of educational materials and just compensation for catechists. A distressing shadow side to this growth in the number of those eligible for catechesis is the increasing difficulty catechists experience in getting parents to enroll their children in the catechetical program and/or to ensure regular attendance in the programs once enrolled. This becomes more problematic the older the children become. Confirmation is still viewed as "graduation" by many. Consequently, an increasing number of those parishes and dioceses that celebrate confirmation in junior high have all but ceased even attempting to provide catechetical programs for high school youth—apart from occasional youth ministry activities.

There is also the issue of time. Put simply, no one seems to have enough of it—the parish DRE, the volunteer catechists, the children and youth we expect to participate, the parents whose support and involvement we need. Catechetical programming must compete with a host of other, often more appealing interests and opportunities that clamor for the time and attention of today's children and their parents. This becomes even more complicated in light of shifting family structures that involve more and more single parents, families in which both parents work outside the home, families in which divorce makes it necessary for children to shuttle back and forth between parents according to a schedule for joint custody.

In view of these and other very real problems the idea of restructuring catechesis to include many small groups, each with its own catechist/facilitator, or the idea of extending the catechetical program to a year-round schedule, or of depending on some form of voluntary participation can seem totally unrealistic. So if we hope to demonstrate that the paradigm shift we are proposing is even worth considering, much less implementing, we need to address these legitimate concerns.

Before we present some specific responses to these concerns, however, we need to first consider a few principles that should underpin any attempt to implement the proposal. We also need to examine certain changes that have been taking place in the ecclesial community and society that can give us additional perspective on the task of making such a paradigm shift in our catechetical structures.

## PRINCIPLES

The first and most important principle affecting any implementation is this: *We must first begin to understand the nature and goal of catechesis in terms of discipleship and discipleship formation.* The rationale and the validity of our premise—that the relational model is the best way to structure our catechesis in the future—presupposes that understanding. If, despite our rhetoric, we continue to think of catechesis primarily in terms of achieving more cognitive goals, then it will seem foolhardy even to consider moving from the more academic structures now in place. On the positive side, if we succeed in making that shift, our approach to certain problems shifts also. For example, we may not find it as difficult to recruit catechists if we no longer think of them primarily as religion teachers.

The second principle to keep in mind is that *we need experimentation and adaptation.* We are not proposing some full-blown, "written in stone" template for restructuring catechesis to be uniformly implemented by every parish in every city in every part of the country. We are proposing a philosophy, if you will, or a general approach to restructuring catechesis that is marked by certain key characteristics or qualities. Translating (incarnating?) this general approach into a concrete program in any given parish allows for a wide range of variations to be dictated by the unique circumstances, resources, and limitations of that parish. We anticipate, therefore, the need for research, experimentation, and collaboration within the catechetical community. This must take place before we can begin to identify with confidence specific forms that might work best in small rural parishes, for example, or before we determine the best ways for implementing this structure in large, suburban parishes. This commitment to the research and experimentation required for creating and adapting our catechetical structures along more relational lines is an essential element of our catechetical agenda for the third millennium.

## CHANGES IN THE ECCLESIAL COMMUNITY AND SOCIETY

Veteran catechists can argue with some justification that we did a great deal of experimenting along the lines we are suggesting back in the late 1960s and throughout the 1970s, and for the most part those experiments faded away. Why should we spend the time and energy to do it again? In response to such objections we wish to say only this: *Times are different.* Those first attempts to shift from the academic to more relational or small-group models were examples of an "idea born before its time." The environments within the church and within society were not yet ready to support such a shift. It is our contention that the adoption of a more relational model in structuring our catechesis is now an idea whose time *has* come. We will offer several "signs of the times" to support this observation.

Vatican II initiated a revolution in how the church understands itself. Karl Rahner called it the second great revolution in the church's history, the first being Paul's insistence that the community accept Gentiles into its midst. The full implications of the revolution begun by Vatican II are finally beginning to seep into the church's consciousness. At the same time we must admit that some strong resistance remains that seeks to thwart the acceptance and implementation of the insights spawned by the council. Nevertheless, this new consciousness is deepening, and its impact on the church's institutional structures, its internal life, and its mission is growing.

We can be especially grateful for the dedicated and scholarly work of the women theologians who have emerged since the council; their work is bringing about one of the most significant of these shifts in the church's consciousness. They have courageously exposed the limiting and harmful effects that the all-pervasive patriarchal model has had on the church in all aspects of its life: its institutional structures for organizing and governing the community, its understanding of priesthood, its interpretation of scripture, its choice of theological images and metaphors, its liturgical and sacramental life. They have challenged the view that the church is rightfully male dominated. They have refuted the presumption that a certain monarchical or hierarchical ordering of the community—with the positions of authority being held exclusively by ordained males—is proper to its nature. In place of that model these theologians have been reclaiming the image put forth by Vatican II—the church is the people of God, a holy people, a priestly people. They demonstrate that the people of God is best understood and organized as a partnership, with neither sex nor any social, ethnic, or political class having any claim to the dominate role. Such an understanding of the church, as Vatican II itself maintained, better reflects what Jesus intended and what the church strove to be in the beginning stages of its life.

The full implications of this shift to an authentically communal way of being church are still unfolding—and strong resistance remains. Yet this break from the grip the patriarchal model has had on the church's consciousness promises to be as liberating for men as it is for women. It promises to have a liberating effect on how the church views society and how it understands and carries out its mission to society, especially in the area of social justice. It promises to alter our understanding of what we are to proclaim when we go forth to proclaim the gospel. It promises to alter how we understand the term *catholic,* whom we should welcome, and how we are to receive them. It promises to alter how we view and relate to other Christian churches and to other world religions. Remember, all of these shifts in our understanding of what it means to be church have been growing from the seeds planted in the documents of Vatican II.

Though it may be some time before we begin to experience the full effects of this new understanding of church, the fact remains that this new consciousness has indeed begun to take root. The point we wish to stress in the context of this study is that this new consciousness provides a very fertile and receptive environment for initiating a more relational model for doing catechesis. To the degree that the church understands itself as essentially communal (and hence relational), it will readily see the value of employing a more relational model in its task of preparing its children and all new members for life and responsible membership in this community. In short, the time is much more propitious for introducing the small-group model for structuring our catechesis than it was forty years ago.

Also included in this shift in the church's consciousness is an element we have been alluding to throughout this work: *discipleship*. We have made the point, of course, that formation in discipleship is being reclaimed in all recent catechetical documents as the rightful goal of catechesis. Equally important, this awareness of our call to be disciples in a community of disciples is finding its way back into the consciousness of the community at large. We see the term used with ever greater frequency by bishops in their official documents. It is finding its way back into the celebration of the sacraments and into homilies, and it is becoming a dominant theme in much of today's spiritual writing. This is not some semantic shift in popular piety. It reflects a major theological shift in the church's self-understanding, one firmly rooted in the gospels. It can be traced in part to the church's rediscovery of the central role of scripture in its life, another fruit of Vatican II. This renewed understanding of discipleship is in perfect harmony, of course, with the shift to a communal or partnership model of church.

Awareness of one's call to discipleship naturally focuses our attention on our relationship to Jesus and on our relationship to one another. It regards learning the truths of the faith from a different perspective, as one of various tasks of discipleship, and not as the sole or even primary requirement of becoming a good member of the community. Again, the point we wish to stress here is that this very real shift in the church's self-understanding provides a much more fertile and accepting environment for introducing the proposed relational model for structuring catechesis. The concept has a natural appeal and can be said to resonate with the church's self-awareness in a way it could not do forty years ago.

Finally, the society in which the church exists and ministers is itself experiencing a change in its self-consciousness that also is generating a receptivity to the concept of the small-group or relational model. There is general agreement among psychologists, sociologists, and social historians that feelings of alienation are one of the most common effects of the rapid and wide-spread social changes our world has been experiencing as it struggles to adapt to the post-industrial era we are entering. For example, while today's technology has increased our ability to communicate more rapidly and over longer distances than at any time in the world's history, our sense of being personally connected to others appears to have dropped to an all-time low.

In the Western world, at least, this trend toward a less personal way of relating began to accelerate after World War II. People left farms and rural communities and moved to the larger, more impersonal cities in ever-increasing numbers. As the cities themselves underwent change, many of the older, often ethnic neighborhood communities began to disintegrate. A second kind of migration began, this time to the suburbs, where one's privacy was valued. Social historians have documented many other causes that have been generating the resulting sense of alienation, loneliness, isolation, and rootlessness. The point we want to stress here is this: There now exists in our society a great number of people of all age groups, of both sexes, and of all socioeconomic strata, who are hungering for interpersonal relationships, for a sense of belonging, for some sense of being rooted in a community.

Certainly today's society and the influences shaping its behavior are much more complex than the scenario I am presenting here. Yet the fact remains that a sense of alienation and loneliness is one of the most prevalent and identifiable characteristics found in all segments of our society. This is the society to which the church is called to minister. Therefore it should not stretch one's imagination too far to suggest that most people today are going to be more open to and supportive of the idea of using the small-group or relational model for doing catechetical ministry than they would have been forty years ago.

These changes in the church's and society's self-understanding do not of themselves guarantee that the relational model can be adopted easily in our catechetical programs. Many practical problems confront such a shift in structures, and we will address them next. But these changes in church and society do provide a more receptive environment for introducing this relational model. Consciously to foster interpersonal relationships and to seek to nurture a sense of community is indeed an idea whose time has come.

## QUESTIONS AND ANSWERS

Perhaps the simplest way to examine how to deal with the practical challenges we can anticipate in shifting from an academic to a more relational or small-group model for catechesis is through a series of questions and answers. Once again we must provide a caveat before we start. The "answers" will not provide detailed blueprints for how to proceed in every concrete situation. We present them primarily to demonstrate that none of the obstacles is insurmountable. As mentioned above, there will be need for further research and experimentation. The "answers" given here are intended to indicate possible directions that such research and experimentation might take.

*Isn't this proposed small-group model more suited for adults than for children and youth? Can it be adapted effectively for all age groups?*

As a general response we can say that the fundamental requirement for participating effectively in the small-group structure we are proposing is *the ability to reflect upon and share one's personal experiences in the light of the gospel.* While it is true that this ability increases in keeping with a person's intellectual and psychological development, it emerges in a rudimentary form by the time the individual reaches the age of reason.

At the level of the primary grades this ability is just beginning to emerge. The major focus and goal in this stage, therefore, would be to develop those socialization skills that are foundational to fruitful interaction within a community or small group. We can continue to do much of what we are already doing in our catechetical programs for this age group. Typically, these children are being taught the principles of fair play and taking turns, the importance of sharing supplies and cooperating in carrying out tasks, the rules of politeness, the need to be sensitive and caring when another is hurting, the need to forgive and reconcile. These skills lead quite naturally to the ability to function effectively in a small-group or in a community setting. Also, our present catechesis in this stage, including that dimension designed to prepare the children for first Eucharist, tends to be far less academic in nature and does not attempt to introduce abstract concepts too soon. It focuses instead on the use of stories, pictures, songs, and creative activities that illustrate the truths of our faith.

So, at the primary level we anticipate very little if any need for change in shifting to the proposed relational model. Our present catechesis at this level is already appropriately relational. In terms of content, we recommend that we begin to introduce the concept and vocabulary of discipleship more conscientiously. Apart from that, we could in most instances proceed with "business as usual."

By about age ten most children are sufficiently developed to begin *to reflect upon and share personal experiences in the light of the gospel*. Traditionally, this is the point at which we tend to introduce the academic model in earnest—and the time the children begin to show the first tentative signs of resistance to and disenchantment with our catechesis. We are suggesting, then, that we can and should begin to introduce the small-group format at this point, appropriately adapted to the children's still limited capacity to reflect and share. It is worth noting that various forms of the small-group model have been used effectively for several decades with this age group in helping them deal with various traumas, such as divorce, the death of a parent, and the like. This clearly demonstrates that children at this age can indeed begin to reflect upon and share their experiences with one another for mutual benefit and growth.

Assuming the small-group model is introduced by around age ten, the children will have become quite familiar and comfortable with its processes by the later middle school or junior high years, when their capabilities to reflect and share are approaching more adult levels. By junior high and throughout the teen years youth can function quite effectively within the small-group model. Our experience has been that it is usually desirable to form youth into same-sex groups throughout the early teens. Given the inherent ambivalence and confusion that is characteristic of "boy-girl" relationships during this stage, both sexes find it easier (read: safer) to share in same-sex groups.

Thus, in answer to the first question, we can say that the small-group model can be adapted effectively for all age groups.

*If we were to no longer consider participation in the catechetical program mandatory, can we expect to maintain attendance?*

It may seem naive to assume we can maintain attendance in our programs on a strictly voluntary or invitational basis. In point of fact, participation in our present programs is already voluntary. Though parents and godparents assume the responsibility to educate the child in the faith at baptism, there is nothing in canon law or elsewhere that says they have the obligation to enroll the child in a Catholic school or the parish's catechetical program. It remains their free choice to decide how best to fulfill their duty. And, although it is true that the community can establish certain norms to determine the child's preparedness to receive first Eucharist or to be confirmed, and can offer programs to help achieve that readiness, it cannot mandate how this preparation is ultimately to be accomplished.

Even though participation in our present catechetical programs is therefore already voluntary in the canonical sense, the manner in which many parishes promote and operate the programs creates the impression that they are mandatory and that guilt is incurred by the parents and/or the children when they fail to participate. It is also a fairly common to create the impression that failure to enroll in the first Eucharist or confirmation program will in itself make the child ineligible to receive the sacrament.

Finally, children in our society are required to go to school. The academic aura of most of our present catechetical programs reinforces the impression that attendance is mandatory. Thus, even though our present catechetical programs are not mandatory, strictly speaking, in most cases they are coated with a veneer of mandatory attendance.

If we were to move away from the academic model toward the concept of an apprentice program for discipleship, one provided in a small-group setting, this in itself would lead parents and children to reexamine their present motives for attendance. Just as discipleship itself is rooted in an invitation that a person remains free to accept or reject, so participation in the disciples' apprentice program must be rooted in an invitation freely accepted. Participation in the program would cease to be mistakenly regarded as an often burdensome academic requirement, a process of "jumping through certain obligatory hoops" on the way to a sacrament (itself too often viewed as a kind of "merit badge"), or as a required course of study that ends in a kind of "graduation" from any further obligation to "attend school."

To effect the shift to a truly voluntary program and at the same time maintain attendance, we will need to attend to three tasks. *First*, we must find ways to help parents grasp the renewed understanding of the nature of discipleship as the core of what it means to be Catholic. *Second*, we need to relate our invitation to participate in the catechetical program to the invitation to discipleship contained in baptism. *Third*, we need to devise ways to extend that invitation in as personal or one-to-one manner as possible.

The first task is certainly the most challenging. It is also the most critical or foundational since it goes to the heart of the paradigm shift we are trying to bring about. We need to explain to parents (and to older youth and the parish community at large) in a clear and compelling way that knowing the truths of our faith, though integral to what it means to be Catholic, is a subsidiary characteristic, not the primary characteristic. Our relationship to Jesus and living out that relationship within the community of disciples are the primary characteristics of "being Catholic."

This will often involve a significant conversion, a letting go of time-honored presuppositions. It will be a task akin to the "new evangelization" the *GDC* speaks about as so necessary in our ministry to many of today's younger Catholics. On the positive side, this understanding of what it means to be Catholic will make much more sense to today's young parents, for many of whom the truths of the faith to which they were exposed in their own catechesis seem to have little relevance at present. They tend to value relationships and seem quite ready to bring basic gospel values to bear on problems and injustices they encounter in today's society. They tend to show little interest in creedal formulas and what they consider outdated institutional practices. So to be told that catechesis is not so much about truths as developing a

93

relationship with Jesus and the community may not seem as radical as it would have just a few decades ago.

We are not prepared to offer specific strategies for promoting this understanding among parents. These will have to be developed through experimentation and adapted to the circumstances of the individual parish. But we are confident that to the degree that we can promote this renewed understanding of the true nature of what it means to be Catholic, parents will be able to recognize for themselves the potential value our catechetical apprentice program has for their children and consequently why it is important for them to participate in it.

What do we mean by the second task, that is, the need to relate our invitation to participate in the catechetical program to the invitation to discipleship contained in baptism? The answer becomes clear when we review the nature and meaning of baptism. For adults who proceed through the RCIA, baptism signifies their free, conscious, definitive, and public acceptance of Jesus' invitation to discipleship. It irrevocably unites them with Jesus *as his disciples* in an ineffable, grace-filled union. It marks their official initiation into the *community of disciples,* the church. Their confirmation, in turn, signifies the completion of the apprentice stage of this discipleship by empowering and commissioning them to participate fully in the community's life and mission.

Baptism for infants contains the same significance, insofar as it establishes them as disciples, bound to Jesus in a grace-filled union, and initiates them into the community. But it is hardly a free, conscious, or definitive acceptance of discipleship by the infant. Its meaning and any *concrete* effect it will have on how the child actually thinks and behaves as an adult rest in the promise made by parents, godparents, and the community to apprentice the developing child in the knowledge, behaviors, and skills of discipleship. Thus, on the one hand, we need to present to parents this understanding of baptism; on the other hand, we need to present the catechetical program precisely as the kind of apprenticeship they have promised to provide. They need to be helped to realize that though baptism publicly and officially identifies the

94

infant as a disciple of Jesus and establishes a mysterious bond between the child and Jesus, in and of itself baptism has no "magic power" to transform the child's thinking or behavior patterns into those of a disciple of Jesus. The foundations for that lifelong process are precisely what we seek to provide through our catechetical apprenticeship.

Promoting this understanding of baptism is, of course, closely connected to efforts to promote the more basic understanding of discipleship itself as the core characteristic of what it means to be Catholic. The two understandings go hand in hand and complement each other. They lie at the heart of the "new evangelization" of which the GDC speaks. The parents' preparation for the baptism of their first child, if done patiently and properly, can be an especially fruitful time for this "new evangelization."

Third, we need to make the invitation to participate in the catechetical program as personal as possible. The rationale for this is rooted in the very nature of discipleship, which always involves a personal invitation to follow Jesus, and in the dynamics of human relationships. In terms of human dynamics a personal invitation conveys two important messages: that I am valued, and that they believe I have something to contribute. It also says that the occasion must have some special value to merit the trouble of extending a personal invitation.

This is certainly not some new insight to veteran catechists. They are well aware that a personal invitation is more effective and desirable than an impersonal written notice. The problem, they point out, is one of logistics—the amount of time and personnel required to extend such personal invitations. Several factors can help make this task seem less daunting. First, such an invitation does not need to be extended anew each year once the program is established. Remember, we are suggesting a more or less continuous program, not one that ends each spring and must be reinitiated each fall with a new round of recruitment. Most groups will be expected to remain together over several years, perhaps longer. Second, since we would not be confined to an academic year, the formation of the initial groups can take place over a more extended period of time. Not every group has to start in September, for example. Groups can be formed at any time. The exception might be in the primary level, where preparation for first Eucharist takes place. But attendance in programs at the primary level is seldom a problem. Third, the catechist/facilitator for each group ideally would be actively involved in inviting the children/youth who are to make up his or her group. Typically, no one would have to make personal contact with more than eight to twelve families.

Such observations do not resolve all the problems connected with attempting to extend personal invitations, but they do demonstrate that a move from an academic model to a small-group model allows us more room for creativity in the task of "recruitment." In the same vein, the above observations regarding how we might effect the overall shift from mandatory to more voluntary participation in the catechetical program do not guarantee a solution to all the problems of maintaining attendance. They do demonstrate, however, that such a shift is far more feasible (and desirable) than it might first seem.

*Given the great difficulty we already experience in trying to find enough volunteer catechists, where can we hope to find the even greater number that would be required if we tried to structure the program along the lines of a small-group model?*

The two biggest (and most legitimate) obstacles we face in recruiting catechists in our present academically structured catechetical programs are (1) feelings of inadequacy as a teacher, and (2) lack of time. The shift to the small-group model does not totally remove these obstacles, but it does tend to render them far less formidable. Let us deal with each in turn.

As long as we remain in fact if not in theory committed to an academic model, catechists are essentially religion teachers. This presupposes two thing: they have an adequate grasp of the information they are to impart, and they have the teaching skills required for doing so effectively. Most parishioners, especially young adults, who make up the pool of potential volunteer cate-chists tend to feel very inadequate on both counts. Nor do most feel they have the additional time needed to be adequately trained for the task.

In the small-group model, however, catechists are not teach-ers. They are group facilitators, and they are co-learners. Most adults already have some experience in functioning in small groups. Many are already members of one small group or another. Also, today's work place often employs the small-group model and uses the principles of group dynamics in its meetings, plan-ning sessions, and training programs. So the concept is already familiar to most of our potential catechists, and many have a great deal of practical experience with it. As facilitators they do not have to be "experts." They may bring more experience to the group about what it means to be a disciple, but they are not expected to know it all or to try to impose their view on the others. Their main task is to guide reflection. Ultimately, it is the Spirit who provides the enlightenment within the group. There are no complicated lesson plans to be developed each week, each requiring special teaching techniques to implement. The overall session format remains the same for each gathering. The basic techniques for facilitating a small group also remain the same for each session. Discipline is seldom a problem in small groups, so there are no special skills to be acquired here. Also, since atten-dance is voluntary, one can expect a higher level of motivation to participate and to contribute. Nor does one have to achieve cer-tain goals or cover a certain number of topics according to a strict academic time table. There are certain goals to strive for and cer-tain topics to deal with in a more or less orderly fashion, but in the small-group model the group sets the pace and is free to take as much time as it needs to explore a given topic. Remember, the overall goal is growth in one's relationship to Jesus as his disciples, not just mastery of certain truths.

The small-group model gives us a whole new understanding of the role of volunteer catechists that affects how we approach their recruitment. It is a role that, though it still has its challenges and still requires some training, will seem much more doable and appealing to our potential recruits. Much of its appeal lies in the nature and benefits of the small-group format itself. Bonds of affection will form between the catechist and the catechized. A sense of community develops. The group becomes a source of emotional as well as spiritual support and growth. All this is especially true when the group stays together over a period of several years. The catechist's role is that of a more experienced or mature member of a little faith community, not a teacher or task master required to impart a certain amount of information and skills to disinterested students in a limited amount of time.

This brings us to the question of time, the second major obstacle we face in recruiting catechists. Research in volunteerism indicates that people will find the time to volunteer if three criteria are met. First, they need to feel they are capable of doing what is asked. Second, they must consider the work important enough to sacrifice their time. Third, the task has to be enjoyable and rewarding—as opposed to tedious or frustrating. Facilitating a catechetical group meets all three criteria. As just demonstrated above, our volunteers have the necessary skills. For any person of faith it is not difficult to explain the importance of our ministry, namely, striving to share that faith with the next generation. Finally, unlike the often tedious and frustrating experience of attempting to "teach religion" to a disinterested class of children or youth, participating in a small group can be both enjoyable and rewarding. Being able to meet these three criteria does not of itself guarantee an adequate pool of volunteer catechists. But it does promise to make the task of recruitment both easier and more successful than it would be using the present academic model.

One other important point to consider in this approach is that it will be much easier for a volunteer facilitator to find a substitute if he or she cannot make a particular session. It is typically much easier to find a friend (or spouse) willing to facilitate a group for a session or two than it is find a person willing to "teach a class."

*Doesn't the small-group model make scheduling more difficult?*
*And is year-round or continuous programming even realistic?*

Scheduling basically involves deciding who meets, when they meet, and where they meet. In the academic model participants are grouped according to grade level. A central location is used for all the classes to meet, and the classes typically gather at a set time each week. Variables include the number of classes needed at any given grade level, the number of classroom facilities the parish can provide at any one time, and the days and times these facilities are available each week. Though one must work within these constraints, this approach is relatively simple and assures a certain uniformity.

Though the small-group model is not nearly so neat, it does provide a great deal more flexibility. In terms of grouping, though participants in a group need to have a certain affinity in terms of intellectual and psychological development, we can cross grade levels in forming our groups. For example, ten- to twelve-year-old children typically can function quite well together in a group regardless of their grade in school. We do not need classroom facilities for meeting. Basically all that is required for meeting is a space that can be made reasonably comfortable and is free of outside distractions. Groups can be formed by neighborhood, for example, and meet in someone's home. No special equipment is needed except perhaps occasional access to a VCR and/or TV, something already available in most households. Finally, each group can be given a great deal of autonomy in deciding the most convenient time for it to meet. There is no need for all groups to meet at the same time and on the same day each week.

In fact, once groups are formed and facilitators are in place, the parish DRE need not be concerned about scheduling unless someone asks for specific help. Each group can do its own scheduling, deciding for itself how it will deal with the Christmas holidays, for example. Also, given the very nature and process of the small-group format, occasional absences by individuals due to illness, a family vacation, or some other personal matter create no special problems for the individual, the facilitator, or the group as a whole. There is no need to "make up" classes. Assuming most

99

groups will remain together for several years, they can adjust the time and place for meeting among themselves as the circumstances of the members change from year to year.

The other question related to scheduling is that of year-round programming. Some background may be helpful here. The academic year developed to meet the needs of the many farm families whose children were needed in the summer months to help plant, cultivate, and harvest crops. Now less than 3 percent of the population in the United States lives on farms, and modern machinery has reduced the number of workers required.* For that reason (among others) many educational theorists are now advocating year-round schooling or at least a much longer school year, claiming that in industrialized countries the academic year is an artificial and unnecessary construct. The suggestion continues to be met with great resistance. So the issue of year-round programming for catechesis is indeed a problem if we continue to tie our catechesis to the academic year.

However, if we can remove catechesis from the academic model and define it as a disciples' apprentice program that takes place in a small-group setting, year-round or continuous programming will seem quite normal. The very nature of the small-group model implies the development of intentional, supportive, small communities. As anyone who has participated in such a support or interest group knows, the rationale and motivation for meeting regularly has its source within the group itself. As long as participants' needs are being satisfied or they are making progress toward the agreed-upon goals, they will be willing to meet year round. As we know, the principles of pedagogy are at work in structuring the academic year. Certain goals are set for the students, a time limit is established for achieving them, and some test to measure students' success marks the end of the term.

------

*In 1893, 42 percent of the population lived on farms. In 1982, 3 percent of the population lived on farms. The percentage is even lower at present (Source: USDA, *Agriculture Fact Book* 1999, June 2000).

In the small-group model, however, it is the group's inner dynamics not an external, artificially determined schedule that determines when it is time to "take a break," to set new goals, and even to dissolve altogether.

## CONCLUSION

This review of the practical problems we face in catechesis was intended to demonstrate how a shift in our approach to catechesis can give us a fresh approach to many of these problems. We did not attempt to solve these problems in any definitive way, but we hope we have shown that the obstacles we can anticipate are not insurmountable. With sufficient creativity and experimentation the transition to a small-group, year-round program is not just desirable but possible.

# 6

# Implications for Methodology

## INTRODUCTION

Changing to a catechesis of discipleship requires a shift not just in how we structure our catechetical programs but also in how we approach our methodology. Since the catechesis of discipleship involves effecting an ongoing *conversion* (see *GDC*, art. 53) that embraces the whole person, our methodology must be rooted in and shaped by an understanding of the nature of conversion and the conversion process.

In fairness it must be stated that the present way we do catechesis within the academic model also implies conversion as its goal. Shaped by the *GCD* published in response to Vatican II, it aims at fostering a "faith ever more conscious, living and active," thus a dynamic faith that continues to grow and to effect changes in how one lives. However, as we will see, because our present catechesis, often unintentionally, continues to be shaped and influenced by the goals and methodology of a catechesis that developed in response to the Reformation, its understanding of conversion and the conversion process also remains rooted to a large degree in that more traditional approach to catechesis.

First, therefore, let us review the nature of conversion in general to ensure a common understanding of the topic. Then we can explore its implications for the methodology we have been employing in our catechesis and the kind of shift in methodology we will need to make if we are to adopt the more relational disciples' apprentice program we have been advocating.

## THE NATURE OF CONVERSION:
## A CHANGE IN CONVICTIONS AND VALUES

*Conversion* means a "thorough turning around" (from the Latin *vertere*, "to turn," and *con*, "completely, thoroughly"); literally, we change directions. Our convictions and our values change. We act or live differently because we come to know and to love differently. We form a new vision of reality, and this enflames us with a new love. Implied here is both a radical, inner (or spiritual) change and a consequent change in the nature of our relationships to and our behavior toward God, other persons, and the material universe.

We can gain insight into the nature of conversion by examining what is involved in changing convictions. To be convinced is to have a truth "conquer" us, overpower us, take possession of us. Stated another way, we surrender to it. A conviction is a truth that becomes an integral part of our person. Quite literally, we "incorporate," or take it into ourselves.

Thus, to be convinced of something is not the same as simply to know it, no matter how comprehensive that knowledge. A few examples may help show this important distinction. When the Big Bang theory was first posited by some scientists, not everyone bought into it. Many scientists came to *know and understand* the theory quite well and were very familiar with mathematical and physical evidence that supported it, but they remained *unconvinced*. They challenged and attempted to disprove the various tenets that supported it. Over time, however, as their challenges were answered, their attempts to disprove it failed, and new evidence was gathered, most scientists did become convinced of its validity—they experienced a conversion. They have now incorporated it into their own worldview and have begun to reexamine previous tenets of physics, astronomy, and cosmology from this new point of view.

We see this same distinction between knowledge and conviction at work in the debate over evolution. Biblical creationists *know* the theory of evolution and the many proofs its adherents use to support it. Yet, they remain *unconvinced*. They remain convinced

103

instead that the biblical account of creation in six days is to be taken literally and view the world from that perspective. In the same vein most conscientious agnostics are quite familiar with the various arguments used to demonstrate the existence of God but obviously remain unconvinced (unconverted).

We are unable to explain with any precision the psychology involved in the transition from knowledge to conviction. It does imply a kind of "leap of faith" at some point, a revelatory (a "removal of the veil") moment when we come to "see" a truth in a new way, a way that overcomes our doubts, redefines who we are, and allows us to look at the rest of reality from a new vantage point.

The point we wish to stress here is that catechesis involves fostering convictions, not simply imparting knowledge and understanding of the truths of our faith. To arrive at a conviction is to experience a conversion. Consequently, the methodology we employ needs to be a methodology of conversion, not a methodology primarily designed to help people acquire more knowledge or understanding. We'll come back to this point shortly.

We can say much the same thing about values. Acquiring a new value and/or rejecting one formerly embraced involves a similar conversion. To acquire a value is to "fall in love." It happens more or less this way. We experience something (a relationship, an action, an object) as a good. It seems to fulfill one or another of our basic needs (for security, affection, aesthetics, self-determination, knowledge, and so forth). In short, it makes us feel happy or fulfilled. Each time we are able to repeat the experience, we discover it has the same effect. At some point we experience conversion. In an intuitive "leap of faith" we begin to value this relationship, this object, or this action. We fall in love with it and give it a place in our value system. It becomes part of who we are. From now on, when we are forced to make choices, this value will play a role, more or less important according to the priority we have given it in our overall value system.

It is important to note that each value takes on the characteristics of a "personal universal." That is, we become convinced that all people could and should value what we value if they only

104

could experience it as we do. We instinctively tend to become evangelists of the things we value, eager to share our "good news" with others, especially loved ones. Finally, it is important to note that it is virtually impossible to argue someone out of a value. Values are born of consistently good experiences and will not be rejected until these are replaced by consistently bad ones. For example, parents can try to convince their daughter that the boy she is in love with is "no good" for her. But until she *experiences* (and acknowledges) harmful effects from the relationship, she will continue to value it. Meanwhile, she will tell her parents, "If you knew him as I do, you'd love him too"—which is the sign of a personal universal at work.

Knowledge in and of itself does not generate values. Values are rooted in experience, and any change of values will likewise be rooted in experience. For example, a person may know all the latest data about the dangers of eating too much red meat. But it is his own dangerously high cholesterol level, not some abstract statistics, that is likely to effect a conversion, that is, change the value he places on eating steak. In much the same way, knowledge about prayer will not of itself lead a person to value prayer. Only by praying and consistently experiencing it as a good does one come to value prayer. Given this understanding of the nature of values, to say that catechesis seeks to effect a conversion in a person's values clearly implies that a methodology primarily designed to impart knowledge will not be effective.

We need to add a few more observations about conversion. Convictions and values are two sides of the same reality. Convictions are essentially cognitive; values are essentially affective. Yet, we will feel passionate about (value) our intellectual convictions, and we will be convinced of (defend intellectually) our affective values. Equally important, because both our convictions and values are integral to who we are—that is, have been incorporated into our very identity as persons—they both define who we are and determine what we do. Deliberately to act contrary to a conviction or value is certainly possible, but to do so is to do a kind of violence to ourselves, to lose something of our integrity. We feel

105

guilt, a certain psychological pain that warns us we are endangering the integrity of our person.

## CONVERSION IN SCRIPTURE:
## RETURNING HOME, LEAVING HOME, STAYING HOME

We find two different kinds of conversion described in the scriptures. The first kind, illustrated by the parable of the prodigal son, is an example of conversion as reconciliation or *returning home*. A person may stray from his or her original convictions and values for a number of reasons—self-indulgence, indifference, a more appealing doctrine. Then something happens, often but not necessarily calamitous, that helps the person "come to his senses," as the parable describes it. A conversion or turning around takes place through which the person "returns home" to those original convictions and values that had been abandoned. This is what most people tend to think of when we speak of conversion—the return of the sinner or lost sheep to the fold. This kind of conversion is found often in the Hebrew scriptures when the Israelites, having strayed from the covenant into idolatry, injustice, or other forms of immorality, come to their senses after some calamity and/or the prompting of a prophet and return to fidelity to the covenant.

A second kind of conversion can be described by the image of *leaving home*. It is best illustrated in the gospel account of the rich young man. He was already living an upright life. His convictions and values were consistent with the conventional religious wisdom of the day. Jesus loved him for that. But Jesus also challenged him to "leave home," to go beyond this conventional wisdom and adopt new convictions and values in keeping with the new vision of God's reign that Jesus was proclaiming. In the Hebrew scriptures we find both Abraham and Moses undergoing this kind of conversion, called by Yahweh to journey to a new place, leaving behind their more primitive religious understandings. The account of Paul's conversion in Acts fits this description as well.

There is third kind of experience, akin to but not actually a conversion, which we also find in the gospels. We can describe it as a *staying home*. It is a pastoral activity that seeks primarily to strengthen and bolster existing convictions and values so people can maintain them in the face of the new challenges (false teaching, persecution, complacency, backsliding, discouragement) they are experiencing or may soon experience. It calls people to grasp more firmly to the rudder of faith, as it were. Much of what we find in the epistles of Paul and the other apostles has this kind of strengthening of convictions as its goal. Its focus is on maintaining the conversion that has already been experienced. The intention behind various portions of both Mark's and Matthew's gospels is similar. The authors are striving to encourage their communities, which have already undergone an initial conversion to discipleship, to hold firm in the face of the persecutions they have begun to experience.

The first kind of conversion just described is a major concern in pastoral ministry, of course. The church continually seeks to promote reconciliation, to call and welcome individuals back from their errant ways.

The primary concern of the church's evangelizing ministry, however, is to effect the second kind of conversion described above. Evangelization is intended to call people to leave their present "home" and to follow Jesus. Our catechesis is intended to continue that process. It also calls upon people to "leave home," to move beyond that initial experience of conversion to Jesus and their initial Christian convictions and values, as good as these are. It is intended to challenge people to continue to grow, to enter more fully and passionately into their relationship to Jesus, to respond more fully to the challenges contained in the gospel, to let go of accurate but still underdeveloped understandings of God, justice, prayer, the nature of the church, and the church's mission in order to acquire new, more mature, more passionately held convictions and values in all these areas.

The effort to protect and maintain one's existing relationship to Jesus and to strengthen existing Christian convictions and values in the face of challenges and threats—the third experience described above—became a major pastoral concern of the church at the time of the Reformation. To some extent this concern has continued up to the present day. The importance given to this pastoral activity almost immediately began to influence the church's approach to catechesis as well. Rather than helping people "leave home," catechesis began to focus on helping people "stay home." Consequently, it adopted methodologies designed to bolster existing faith. It began to avoid and even view as dangerous methodologies that might encourage people to "leave home." We contend that despite the efforts to achieve catechetical renewal since Vatican II, much of our catechesis continues to employ methodologies better suited to maintaining our faith. Such catechesis may hinder rather than foster the kind of conversion catechesis is intended to evoke. So let us turn now to the issue of methodology as it related to these various kinds of conversion and test this premise.

## THE CONVERSION PROCESS
## AND CATECHETICAL METHODS

Conversion, whether in the terms of reconciliation or in terms of adopting a new conviction or value, is ultimately beyond our control. There is no guaranteed "brainwashing" strategy we can use. We can only provide certain conditions, experiences, and opportunities. The actual experience of conversion involves an inner conversation among God's grace, our intellect, and our free will. In short, conversion is always a graced moment, and as the scriptures state, no one can say "Jesus is Lord" except by the Spirit's prompting.

Fortunately, we can look to Jesus' ministry, which was continually directed toward effecting conversion, to discern the outlines of a methodology of conversion. His strategy was actually quite simple. Jesus had a capacity to evoke in people the need to reflect upon and reexamine their own experiences, convictions, and values in the light of his own Wisdom-shaped vision. He did this first of all by his words, the best example being his parables. Volumes have been written on the nature of parables and their effectiveness for presenting open-ended questions, presenting a new and often surprising and radically different slant on familiar

108

topics, and challenging the conventional wisdom of the time. His straightforward teaching, such as the Sermon on the Mount and the many aphorisms scattered throughout the gospel narrative, has much the same effect.

His actions also had this effect. Not just his miracles—though they must have had a profound influence on the people privileged to witness them. More often it was the way he treated those he encountered that evoked reflection. He welcomed the social outcasts of his day, he violated taboos governing how men and women should associate in public, he challenged religious authority figures. At the same time he showed great reverence for the Temple, observed the religious feasts, went off for long periods of time to pray. He trusted totally in Yahweh's providence for his "daily bread." He shunned violence and did not seek political power. Thus, through his actions and his example, he challenged much of the conventional wisdom and many of the social norms of his day, stimulating in others the need to reevaluate their own convictions and values.

Jesus' simple methodology of conversion, which starts with and respects people's experience and leads them to reflect upon it in the light of his good news, has been adopted and systematized, as it were, in the process we have come to know in catechetical circles as *praxis*. It is as old as the church itself, as Tom Groome demonstrates.[1] It was most effectively reclaimed, developed, and adopted as a catechetical method in our time by the church in Latin America. We can also recognize its elements in the methodology used in the restored RCIA. By way of review we will list here the five movements or steps involved as synthesized by Groome:

1. State what is—name our present experience.
2. Critically and creatively explore this experience, naming the potential for good or evil it seems to contain.
3. Present and examine what the gospel and our tradition have to say about this experience.
4. Compare and contrast (put into dialogue) the evaluation of our present experience and the wisdom of the gospel and our tradition.

5. Form a response (experience a conversion) in which we approach our present experience with the new insights (convictions and values) that have been shaped by this dialogue.[2]

Without consciously doing so, many prayer groups and various support groups use a form of praxis similar to this in guiding their discussion. The classical formula of "see, judge, and act," used so effectively in the Catholic Action movement in the mid 1900s, reflects this same kind of praxis. In fact, all of the church's present convictions and values, summarized in its creedal statements and official documents, in its formal moral code, and in the rituals of its liturgical cult, were arrived at through this kind of praxis.

For example, the early church found itself confronted by the issue of allowing Gentiles into the community uncircumcised. It analyzed the situation and its implications through debate—sometimes quite heated—and also examined it in the light of Jesus' teachings. The community then experienced a conversion (a new conviction) in which it came to understand the Gentiles, itself, and its mission in a totally new light.

This kind of praxis has been repeated through the centuries and is seen most clearly each time the church gathers in council to struggle with a problem or challenge. The process is seen clearly in Vatican II, which devoted a great deal of time to reflecting on the present situation of church in regard to its relationship to a radically changing society. It brought these insights into dialogue with the scriptures and tradition. This process evoked a true conversion resulting in a new (or renewed) set of convictions regarding the church, its internal life, and its mission.

Unfortunately, as almost forty years of recent history shows us, this conversion experience has been trickling down to the grassroots community slowly and unevenly. And there are those, often in powerful and influential positions in the church, who remain unconverted and continue to resist the change of heart the council has called us to embrace.

In any event, it takes no special insight to recognize that this same basic praxis, appropriately adapted, provides us with a *methodology of conversion* very well suited to the small-group format we are recommending. It is time honored; we can trace its use to Jesus and then to the church throughout its history. And as that history shows, it is effective. We do not intend to give a detailed analysis of "how to do it" here. Much practical information of that sort is already available. Those new to catechesis can find principles of praxis explained and applied in the current teacher's manuals of most religion textbook series. We will, however, sketch out briefly some of elements and some basic principles involved in adapting this process to catechesis within a small-group setting.

Before we outline these elements and principles, however, we need to address a legitimate objection many veteran catechists can raise at this point. It can be said quite emphatically that praxis is hardly a new concept in catechetical circles and also that this methodology has already been adopted and integrated into our present catechetical materials and programs.

In response, we agree that praxis is not a new concept for catechists. However, we challenge the premise that praxis has been integrated into our present programs. *Co-opted* might be a better description. The fact is that most of our programs continue to follow a more or less academic model, with a set curriculum and preestablished goals. This model by its nature does not allow for an authentic praxis.

Typically, the academic model of catechesis is geared to (and also committed to) presenting the *results* of the praxis engaged in by previous generations. In our present academic model the goal is necessarily predetermined: to present and to foster an understanding of the convictions and values of the church as these are expressed in its existing creed, code, and cult. In our context these convictions and values are considered to be summarized especially well in the *CCC*. The curriculum, the lesson plans, and the experiences offered are all shaped by this predetermined goal. While it is a noble goal, it does not allow for authentic praxis. In authentic praxis one can never be quite sure what new convictions and values will emerge or what form they might take.

Thus, while the academic model may in all sincerity go through the motions of praxis and allow students to discuss their own experiences up to a point, the principles of praxis do not drive or shape the dialogue. What ultimately drives and shapes the dialogue are the predetermined goals of the curriculum, namely, knowledge and understanding of certain convictions and values of previous generations of Catholics. Thus, students may come to *know* quite well the convictions and values held by others, but no real *conversion* in their own convictions and values may ever take place. True praxis always leads to new *personal* convictions and values that echo the convictions and values of past generations of disciples but are also uniquely those of this new generation of disciples. If we are doing authentic catechesis by means of authentic praxis, each new generation will "write its own catechism," one that truly echoes rather than simply recites previous catechisms.

So, although we find the language of praxis in our contemporary catechesis, the classroom is not by nature geared to allow it to take place. In our society a classroom is a place we go expecting to acquire some kind of knowledge about certain things. We now have a whole arsenal of very creative and educationally sound techniques and methods for facilitating this learning, including experiential activities and discussion. The principle of "starting where the students are" is considered fundamental to the process. But success is ultimately measured by whether or not the students know the predetermined subject matter at the end of the class or the semester. In the context of a classroom students quickly get conditioned to giving the "right" responses, regardless of their personal convictions. Though time for discussion of personal experiences may be allotted, it is often viewed more as a warm-up or optional activity and will often be preempted if there is "a lot of material to cover."

When praxis was rediscovered and began to be reintroduced to the catechetical community almost thirty years ago, it was eagerly embraced and had the potential to revolutionize the ministry. But, because we still had not changed our understanding of the overall nature and goal of catechesis to focus on discipleship, we continued to use the academic model to shape our programs, and the methodology of praxis has been co-opted by that academic model.

Adopting the small-group or relational model by its nature provides the proper environment for praxis to function authentically. However, the success of praxis as the methodology of conversion depends ultimately on our ability to shift our understanding of the nature and goal of catechesis itself. If faith is viewed dynamically in terms of developing one's relationship to Jesus, and the community of disciples is also viewed as dynamic reality, then praxis can work. It becomes the means through which this generation of the church can arrive at, articulate, and incarnate its own convictions and values about that faith relationship in light of and in dialogue with its own lived experience. That incarnation and articulation, if authentic, will be in harmony with and consequently echo the scriptures and our tradition. But it will also have its own uniqueness, an outcome we cannot expect to predetermine.

As long as the church remains preoccupied with a paternalistic need to protect its members from the dangers of false teaching and is committed to helping them maintain the faith of their ancestors, the methodology of praxis will seem ineffective at best, and dangerous at worst. The more structured, scheduled, preprogrammed, and hence safer nature of the academic approach will be the preferred model. Certain elements of praxis may be introduced and tolerated, but only if control of the outcome can be maintained.

Thus, for this praxis truly to work, we catechists (and the church) will need to exercise two critical virtues. The first is *trust*. We must trust that the Spirit is present in the gathered group. We must trust in the value of the experiences the participants bring to the group because we trust that the Spirit is already active in their lives. We must trust in the power of the word in and of itself to shed light on the real meaning and value of those experiences. Finally, we must trust in the validity and power of the wisdom contained in our tradition. The present articulation of that wisdom may reflect language and metaphors better suited to another time, but the underlying wisdom remains and needs to play a critical role in the dialogue we hope to engender.

The second critical virtue we need to bring to praxis is *patience*. The process by its nature takes time and unfolds according to its own inner logic and the prompting of the Spirit; it cannot be constrained by some artificial schedule. It can be quite "messy" and can often seem to be going nowhere. In short, we cannot pre-program conversion. We need to trust and to be patient, because we have no ultimate control of the process.

## SOME BASIC PRINCIPLES

As mentioned earlier, we do not intend here to give a detailed "how to do it" analysis of the process of praxis for each age level or an exploration the various skills and strategies involved. Much of this kind of information is already available. But we do want to identify some basic principles that affect how we adapt the process to different age groups and different circumstances.

First, praxis always begins with the participants' own experiences. Therefore, we need to remain sensitive to the role the participants' ages and circumstances play in shaping those experiences. Younger children live in a much smaller world—family, school, playmates—and have a much more limited range of experiences. Older youth with more freedom and mobility tend to have a much wider range of experiences.

Likewise, the different stages of psychological and physical development bring with them their own proper experiences. The onslaught of puberty, for example, brings with it a whole range of new experiences that remain quite foreign to younger children. In the same way, circumstances play an important role. The experiences of children living in a small, rural, ethnically homogeneous community are quite different from those of children living in an urban, ethnically diverse community. The group's socioeconomic status is usually an important circumstance also. On the other hand, because modern communication technology has created a kind of "global village," we can anticipate that certain experiences

114

will be common to most groups. Finally, we need to take into account each age group's capacity for reflection and will have to adapt our process accordingly. Younger children require more guidance and structure than older children, for example.

In terms of experiences, there is one other important principle. While all experiences are valid, all experiences do not have equal value in terms of the kind of conversion we may be attempting to foster at a given time. We will sometimes need to provide specially tailored experiences, such as a field trip to a homeless shelter or a carefully chosen simulation exercise, in order to foster the need for reflection on the desired topic.

So, while praxis is a very natural process as such, when used as a method for guiding people to growth in discipleship it does call for some basic knowledge of the group's stage of development and circumstances. Since much of this same kind of information is needed to ensure the effectiveness of the academic model, there is no need for "new research" in these areas.

Another important principle relates to something we have already alluded to and will explore in more detail in a later chapter: inculturation and adaptation. As listed above, the pivotal step in praxis involves effecting a dialogue between the participants' personal experience and the experience of the faith community as this is articulated in scripture and the church's tradition (its creed, code, and cult). Dialogue implies the ability to hear and understand the other's point of view. While both scripture and tradition have validity as they are presently articulated, both reflect the language, imagery, and theological metaphors of particular cultures at particular points in history. In presenting them as a basis for dialogue, they often require some degree of "translation" and exegesis if they are to make sense to this particular group, living in the twenty-first century, possessing language, images, and metaphors that are shaped by its own culture. This adaptation and inculturation of the existing, official articulation of our faith is no easy task, of course. But the catechetical community needs to make a firm commitment to pursue this task if it hopes to use praxis effectively. Though some people will resist the very suggestion, fearful that orthodoxy or true Catholic identity are being jeopardized by the process, we need to keep in mind that this kind of adaptation and inculturation is precisely what we have been called to do by the *GDC*.

The last principle we wish to mention here related to praxis deals with the final movement in the process, namely, the desired conversion, the birthing of a new conviction or value related to discipleship. As stated earlier we ultimately have no control over when or if a conversion actually takes place. Participants remain free to accept or reject the invitation to grow that is contained in the process. This decision may develop slowly over a period of time, perhaps a long time. We can test to see if the participants have acquired some new knowledge or understanding related to our faith, but acquiring knowledge and understanding is no guarantee of a conversion. For that reason, changed attitudes and behaviors are the only true test of the success or failure of our enterprise. It is not always easy to make such observations. Thus, in terms of determining the success of our catechesis, the virtues of trust and patience mentioned above become especially important.

This seems to have been the approach of Jesus in his own ministry. If we are to believe the gospel accounts, his own specially chosen disciples were often very slow learners. He showed great patience in fostering their growth. He respected their freedom and continued to invite rather than to coerce. In this regard perhaps the most important thing for us as catechists to remember about the ministry of Jesus is that he did not expect to see a "finished product" during his short time with his disciples. He realized (and he trusted) that their growth would continue long after the short apprenticeship he provided them.

## CONCLUSION

On the one hand, recommending that we implement the principles of praxis, appropriately adapted to the participants' age and circumstances, as the *methodology of conversion* required for effective catechesis may not seem particularly innovative or radical. Veteran catechists may point out that it has been in use for some time. It is true that we find references to the various principles of praxis and use of its rhetoric in most of today's published catechetical programs. But because the academic model continues to shape both the structure and the goals of catechesis in these programs, we maintain that praxis has in fact been co-opted by educational methodologies more suited to fostering growth in knowledge. G. K. Chesterton once said, "Christianity has not been tried and found wanting; it has been found difficult and not tried." We could well say, in a similar vein, that praxis in relation to contemporary catechesis has not been tried and found wanting but has simply not been tried.

On the other hand, those who decry the loss of Catholic identity and advocate a return to an even more academically structured, systematic, and content-oriented catechesis than we now provide have always been highly critical, if not alarmed by, the concept of praxis. To them it appears at best to be devoid of content, a haphazard, self-absorbed, "feel good" exercise. At worst they believe it leads to highly relative and subjective (and therefore erroneous) interpretations of both scripture and tradition. We can better address the concerns of such critics in a later chapter in which we discuss the whole question of Catholic identity. That is actually the main issue here. For, as we have already suggested and must explore in more detail, how one defines Catholic identity of necessity defines the goal of catechesis and consequently determines the most appropriate methods for achieving that goal.

However, at this point we can say this much to such critics, and also to our veteran catechists who may be concerned that the program and methodology we are proposing risk being too formless and contentless. The disciples' apprenticeship program we are proposing of its nature must have structure and be approached in a systematic way. Ongoing reflection on scripture and our tradition is of necessity at the very core of the process. The program has its roots in the church and the church's catechetical tradition. It seeks to initiate those catechized into the life and mission of that church. Also, praxis properly understood provides a particular philosophy of methodology, a kind of general framework for our catechesis that allows us to incorporate and utilize a wide range of strategies and techniques. By its nature it is quite flexible but not so flexible as to be formless.

As said several times before, if we fully grasp the degree to which our whole catechetical paradigm shifts once we truly make discipleship our goal, then we will be able to appreciate the value of both the small-group structure and the methodology of conversion (praxis) being proposed. As long as our catechetical goal continues, consciously or unconsciously, to be to foster (and maintain) knowledge and understanding of the faith as ends in themselves, we will be suspicious of the small-group structure and praxis. We will continue to gravitate back to the academic model (and academic methods) as the best way to structure and carry out our ministry. Let us now turn to the question of catechesis for adults and explore how the shift to the goal of discipleship affects this aspect of our ministry.

# 7

# Permanent Catechesis,
# New Evangelization,
# and the Adult Community

### INTRODUCTION

Since Vatican II a major objective of catechetical ministry has been to shift from a child-centered focus to a more adult focus. Yet, despite the rhetoric of catechetical documents that so eloquently advocate lifelong learning, the theoretical arguments of scholars who continue to remind us that "Jesus played with children and taught adults," and the dedicated and creative efforts of the practitioners of adult catechesis, we seem to have made little progress in effecting this shift.

There have been occasional success stories in individual dioceses and parishes, but most who are involved in adult catechesis today admit that it remains a very challenging ministry. It remains difficult to awaken or sustain interest. The numbers who actively participate remain small. So do diocesan and parish budgets dedicated to adult catechesis. What, we need to ask, has been the problem?

Actually there have been several problems. First, we have had no tradition to build upon. Prior to Vatican II there was virtually no effort put into adult catechesis. Having learned the truths of the faith in childhood, adults felt there was nothing more to learn. Besides, the laity were not expected to delve into theology or scripture, which were considered the more or less

exclusive domain of the clergy. Thus, after Vatican II adult catechesis was initially viewed and to a certain extent continues to
be viewed as something of a novelty rather than normative for
adult Catholics.

Second, as we have stressed throughout this work, to this
point we have failed to communicate effectively to adults that
the goal of catechesis is discipleship. Because the majority of our
catechesis continues to take place in an academic setting, most
adults presume that the sole goal of catechesis is to acquire
knowledge of the faith. This perpetuates the pre–Vatican II mentality that catechesis is primarily for children. After "graduat-
ing" from childhood, most adults view continuing catechesis as
optional.

The only experience of catechesis for most adult Catholics,
whether for themselves or for their children, continues to be associated with an academic model. We should not be surprised, therefore, that adults regard catechesis for adults as education, no
matter how creatively it is titled and promoted. Nor should we be
surprised that they consider it optional. To be sure, the desire for
economic or career advancement motivates many adults to seek
further education. Also, a large number of adults, who now have
more leisure time at their disposal, pursue specialized educational
opportunities related to personal interests or hobbies. However,
such adult education is also viewed as optional.

It is our premise that until we succeed in firmly establishing
discipleship as the goal of catechesis and cease using the academic
model as the chief means for doing our catechesis, we will never
succeed in shifting from a child-centered catechesis and will be
unable to establish an adult-centered ("permanent") catechesis as
normative. On the other hand, we are also convinced that if we do
succeed in reclaiming discipleship as the overarching goal and
organizing principle of our catechesis, and in the process do break
from the academic model, we will have gone a long way toward
moving from a child-centered to a truly adult-centered catechesis—not just in rhetoric but in practice. We explore the implications of that premise in this chapter.

## DISCIPLESHIP: THE GOAL OF ADULT CATECHESIS

Once we begin to describe the goal of catechesis as discipleship with Jesus and seek to foster growth in discipleship by means of a more relational catechetical model, we are finally able to view and promote adult catechesis in a whole new way. Discipleship, like any personal relationship, is by nature dynamic, open to ongoing growth in both depth and breadth. Like all relationships, discipleship by its very nature must continue to grow or it will cool and eventually die. Also, as we mentioned earlier, there is no "graduation" when one becomes a disciple of Jesus. We never complete the program, as it were, or reach a point where we can strike out on our own, independent of the Master.

As we have seen in the *GDC,* we can distinguish certain stages of growth in discipleship, beginning with initial encounter/conversion and proceeding through an apprenticeship that culminates in full initiation into the community of disciples. Then, as the *GDC* aptly describes it, begins the stage of "permanent catechesis." The apprentice stage, which is actually quite appropriate for children and youth who have been baptized in infancy (and for adult converts involved in the RCIA) is designed to root us firmly in discipleship. Once rooted in our relationship with Jesus, we begin our vocation of discipleship in earnest. This can be described as the ongoing process of striving to walk with, learn from, and participate in the ministry of Jesus. Adult catechesis authentically understood is the lifelong (permanent) process of deepening our relationship with Jesus. As such, it can never be considered optional or a task we "outgrow."

Having said that, we can begin to appreciate that the real challenge of adult catechesis today does not lie in developing new programs for fostering growth in discipleship among adults. As the *GDC* observes, we have many forms of catechesis already (art. 71). Nor does our task lie in finding creative new ways to promote adult participation in these programs. It is actually much more basic. We need to begin by fostering in adults a fundamental awareness that they are called to be disciples. Only then can we expect them to grasp the true nature and importance of adult catechesis as the *GDC* and other catechetical documents have described it.

Unfortunately, the evidence indicates that most adult Catholics today do not yet think of themselves as disciples in the scriptural sense of the term. Nor do they think of the church as the community of Jesus' disciples. For most adult Catholics "community of disciples" remains more a pious description than a theological definition laden with practical implications. This assessment of adult Catholics is not intended to imply guilt, insincerity, or indifference on their part. Yet, as we hope to show by examining the dynamics that have shaped most adult Catholics since Vatican II, fostering a basic sense of awareness of discipleship and of being a community of disciples is our first task in the process of establishing the kind of "permanent catechesis" of which the *GDC* speaks.

## ADULT CATHOLICS TODAY: A BRIEF ANALYSIS

Volumes have been written about the impact Vatican II has had on the church, and scholars continue to explore the subject in all its theological nuances. Yet if we are to understand the change it effected in how most Catholics understand and practice their faith today, we need only focus on one basic issue. Prior to Vatican II most Catholics viewed God's love for them as somewhat *conditional,* a love that had to be earned by following the church's moral teachings and by participating in the church's sacramental and devotional life. Also, church teaching made it very clear that the consequence of failing to gain God's approval was hell—eternal damnation. We should not underestimate how completely these two basic religious beliefs shaped the motivation of Catholics to accept the church's doctrinal teaching and to strive to obey its moral laws prior to the council. Nor should we underestimate the authority this tended to vest in the church's leaders (hierarchy and clergy), to whom the laity looked to determine how best to gain God's approval. Though it was not always acknowledged, in a real sense fear of hell was the operative principle or the glue that held the church together from before the Middle Ages right up to Vatican II.

For most Catholics, then, the most radical and liberating truth promoted by Vatican II was the good news that God loves us *unconditionally.* God's love and mercy are not earned. They are freely given and available to all, including those who are not Christians. Though hell remained a possibility, it now seemed highly improbable to most Catholics that this all-loving and infinitely merciful God would actually condemn well-intentioned people to eternal damnation for occasionally falling prey to human frailties. This simple good news, which seems to resonate so well with our deepest religious instincts, was enthusiastically embraced and very quickly became a central theme of our catechesis and pastoral activity. It also removed almost overnight the underlying motivation of fear that had been prompting most Catholics to believe and follow the church's theological, moral, and religious teachings for so many centuries.

The decline in the "fear motive" probably accounts more than any other factor for the rapid decline in so many of the traditional Catholic practices following the council: the decline in regular Sunday mass attendance, the virtual disappearance of the sacrament of penance in the lives of many Catholics, the decline in popularity of various devotional practices that had long been viewed primarily as means for gaining God's approval. The lack of urgency most new parents began to feel about having infants baptized "as soon as possible" (to the chagrin of many grandparents) also indicated that fear of God's wrath had ceased to be their primary motive for approaching the sacrament. For much the same reason many people ceased to be afraid to follow their own conscience in certain moral matters, even if it meant going against the official teaching of the church's authorities. How most Catholics have dealt with the issue of birth control after Vatican II is perhaps the prime example of the exercise of this newfound freedom to act contrary to official teaching in matters of conscience.

123

Most Catholics embraced the other changes in church life initiated by the Council as well: use of the vernacular at mass, dropping the Friday abstinence, ecumenical overtures extended to other Christian churches, opportunities for the laity to become more involved in the governance of the church (for example, the formation of parish councils), emergence of various lay ministries, and reintroduction of scripture study. We must admit, however, that while such changes were welcomed, the majority of Catholics never fully understood or had explained to them the theological and historical rationale for such changes. What most dominated their new awareness and affected their motivation was the good news of God's unconditional love for them.

To understand today's adult Catholics, we need to point out one other less positive but equally important observation. Either it was never adequately explained or too many Catholics simply failed to grasp the *therefore* that needs to accompany the good news of God's unconditional love for us. Precisely because God loves us so much, we have been called to respond to God's love just as unconditionally by striving wholeheartedly to pursue God's will for us in union with Jesus—precisely as disciples of Jesus. In short, though the motivation changes, our behavior as Catholics after the council should be similar in many ways to what it had been before. For example, we are called to participate in the Eucharist (give thanks) not out of fear of punishment if we miss, but precisely as a grateful community of disciples and in response to God's unconditional love for us. Either way, we are still called to participate. As in the past we are called to practice self-denial today, not to gain God's approval or to earn God's forgiveness but to root out those selfish tendencies that prevent us from loving and caring for our neighbor, as Jesus taught his disciples to do.

It is safe to say, then, that much of the uniformity in belief and practice among Catholics prior to the council had its roots in our fear of God's wrath if we failed to earn his approval. Having set aside that motivation, we have failed thus far to replace it with the desired positive motivation intended by the council, namely, the motivation that is rooted in our discipleship with Jesus. Lacking this common vision and motivation of discipleship, the adult population of the church, at least in the United States, has become divided into rather disparate groupings. The analysis of the Archdiocese of Milwaukee given by Archbishop Weakland in 1998 probably reflects the situation in most dioceses in the United States today.[3]

Archbishop Weakland observed, first of all, two rather polarized groups. At one pole is a small but well-organized and quite vocal group of ultra-conservative Catholics who both reflect and advocate a return to the beliefs and practices of the pre–Vatican II church. At the opposite pole is a small, less-organized but equally vocal group of ultra-liberals, who, though remaining in the church, are calling for extensive and rapid change in all aspects of church life and are highly critical of Rome's resistance to such change.

Between these two poles we find the majority of practicing Catholics today. We can describe them as moderates, though some tend more toward the "right" and others toward the "left." They participate regularly in the life and worship of their parish. Many are quite generous with both their time and their money in supporting church ministry. They have accepted—even though they do not always understand—the rationale behind the various changes in church life introduced since the council. They tend to be respectful and loyal *in principle* to the authority vested in the church's hierarchy and clergy. They tend to be receptive and responsive to much of the church's teaching in areas of social justice, for example. Nevertheless, having enthusiastically embraced the good news of God's unconditional love, they are not intimidated by that authority. They reserve for themselves the right to decide in what they consider matters of conscience, especially in areas of sexual morality.

Many in this group are open to more changes in the church's discipline, such as allowing married clergy and the ordination of women, but do not feel the urgent need to advocate for them in the way the ultra-liberal group does. They have already witnessed some rather dramatic changes in church teachings and practices that they had long been led to consider unchangeable: Friday abstinence; liberalization in the granting of annulments; the involvement of laity, and in particular women, as lectors and eucharistic ministers; the church's stance toward evolution; the move away from the literal to an exegetical approach in interpreting scripture; and so on. Because they did not fully understand the rationale for changing teachings and practices that they had been taught to believe were unchangeable, many Catholics mistakenly began to view all church doctrine as relative. Though the term *cafeteria Catholic* is much too pejorative a description for them, implying as it does a faith of convenience, many of the adults in this middle group no longer take much interest in any but the most fundamental doctrinal issues.

There are two other groups who, though baptized Catholics are now more or less alienated from the church. One of these is the large group of young adults who have simply dropped out. Though many in this group are sympathetic to and are often living by basic gospel values, they feel neither the need nor the desire to participate in the church's sacramental or ministerial life. A smaller group is composed in large part of Catholics who once belonged to the ultra-liberal group. A significant number of women also belong to this group. They have basically given up on the church's willingness or ability to implement the changes they believe were called for by Vatican II. Some are fending for themselves. Others have joined other Christian churches to be nurtured.

Finally, as Archbishop Weakland noted, we must also recognize the ethnic pluralism that exists in most dioceses today. Though the majority of Catholics in the United States can still trace their ancestry to western and central Europe, the number of American Catholics of Hispanic, Asian, or Pacific Rim origins is increasing rapidly.

The above analysis is somewhat simplistic. A number of thorough scientific studies have been done in recent years that can provide much more detailed and nuanced information about the adult church, broken down by age groups, gender, ethnic background, and geographic regions. Yet in terms of any attempt to vitalize adult catechesis in the third millennium and to make it normative, we believe that our analysis enables us to identify the core tasks we will need to address. Let us look at these next.

## ADULT CATECHESIS: CORE TASKS FOR THE THIRD MILLENNIUM

Our focus here will be on the large middle group we described above, adults of good will who remain loyal and at least somewhat active within the church, adults convinced of God's unconditional love for them but not yet adequately aware of the radical nature of the discipleship to which that love calls them. Because this group is still "in touch" with the church, it is the one we will have the greatest opportunity to influence through our existing ministry and the structures presently available to us.

To begin, it should now be clear that the decline among most adult Catholics of fear and consequent submission to authoritarian pronouncements has removed one of their primary and long-standing motivations for participation in the life and work of the church. Therefore, we will have to awaken in its place a new kind of motivation, one understood as our free response to God's unconditional love. Put simply, our first task in vitalizing adult catechesis today is to help adult Catholics complete this sentence: *God loves us totally and unconditionally; therefore we should...*

It is in the death and resurrection of Jesus that God's unconditional love for us is most fully revealed. It is also in Jesus' example of unwavering trust and total dedication to God's will that we find the "therefore" part of the sentence most fully revealed to us. Thus, it is by identifying with Jesus that we can most fully recognize and experience God's love for us. Through that same identification we can also most fully and authentically respond to that love. In this light, here is how we need to help today's adult Catholics complete the above sentence: *God loves us totally and unconditionally; therefore we should strive with all our strength to be committed disciples of Jesus.* To help adults understand and accept that simple statement is our first and most fundamental task in adult catechesis today. Properly understood and embraced,

127

that statement can awaken the desired new motivation for adults to want to participate freely and fully in the life and work of the church—and by extension to participate in permanent catechesis.

The second task flows from and is closely related to the first. We need to help adult Catholics, once they recognize their own vocation as disciples, also to recognize the church as the *community of Jesus' disciples.* As such, the church exists not just to celebrate and sustain the faith of its members and to care for their needs, though those are certainly essential elements of the church's nature. Just as important, however, the church exists as a community in mission, empowered and commissioned to proclaim and give witness to the risen Lord and to the reign of God being established through the working of God's Spirit. Thus, as individual disciples we participate in the church's efforts to walk with and learn from Jesus (we strive to celebrate and sustain our faith) precisely so we will be able to better participate in the church's mission of bringing the good news of God's unconditional love to all humanity and with it the sure hope for the coming of God's reign. Thus, our authentic Catholic response to God's unconditional love needs to go beyond simply rejoicing in it to striving to bring the same good news to others by the witness of our words and, more important, through the witness of our works of healing, forgiveness, reconciliation, justice, and peace.

It should be noted that neither of these tasks involve us in complex theology or subtle doctrinal distinctions that would require carefully planned formal education programs. It is primarily a matter of helping Catholic adults build upon and draw logical conclusions from the truth they have already enthusiastically embraced, namely, God's unconditional love for them as revealed in Jesus. It involves helping them take the next step in completing the renewal begun by Vatican II.

It should be further noted that experience demonstrates that those adults who do make that next step and become firmly rooted in discipleship and in the church's life and mission will instinctively engage in permanent catechesis. They quite naturally seek more doctrinal precision whenever they discover that their present understanding is no longer adequate to explain their experience. They have also demonstrated the ability to recognize the value and to appreciate the meaning contained in the church's tradition. In the process they have shown great creativity in applying that meaning, if not the external or literal elements of the tradition, to the new situations they are encountering today. Is not this kind of ongoing learning exactly what permanent catechesis hopes to achieve?

By saying that our two tasks are simple in nature does not imply that they will be easy to carry out. In fact, it will probably take another generation to do so. Ironically, at this point in time one of the most fruitful ways to promote this awakening of faith in Catholic adults is to pursue the kind of renewal in the catechesis of young people advocated in earlier chapters. We cannot hope to shift the goal and focus of catechesis for children and youth to discipleship without explaining the nature and rationale of that shift to their parents, to catechists, and to the rest of the adult community. The same is true if we are to succeed in making the shift from the academic model to a more relational model. So, though attention may for a time seem to be primarily on children and youth, this focus provides a perfect opportunity and vehicle for communicating to adults their own call to discipleship and their mission as a community of disciples. If done properly, the renewal of catechesis for children and youth can have a profound impact on the adult community as well.

It is also safe to presume that once the first generation of children and youth has been properly apprenticed and fully initiated into the community of disciples, its members will recognize their need for permanent catechesis. At that point all the foundations will have been laid for establishing adult or permanent catechesis as an integral and normative part of the church's life. And we will have finally completed the renewal of catechesis (and of the church) envisioned by Vatican II.

Another ally we already have in place that can help awaken the desired sense of discipleship in our adults is the RCIA process. In parishes truly committed to it the RCIA not only apprentices the converts in discipleship but also stirs up among the members of the parish community a new appreciation of their own baptism and the responsibilities of their own discipleship. The transforming effect the RCIA can have on an entire parish should never be underestimated. Therefore, we would do well to continue to strive to make it an integral part of parish life and should also consider it an essential part of our effort to vitalize adult catechesis and promote the concept of permanent catechesis.

Another program already in place that can be an invaluable aid is the parish's baptism preparation program for new parents. To date, in many parishes it still tends to be under-utilized, is presented in a perfunctory manner, and is too often little more than a "walk through" of the ceremony. Yet it has great potential as a means for new evangelization and for awakening in the young adults, godparents, and in many cases grandparents a new appreciation for their own baptism and their own call to be disciples of Jesus. Thus, as catechists concerned for adult catechesis, we need to make the parish baptism program a top priority. It needs to be designed (redesigned) with great sensitivity and creativity, both in terms of content and methodology. It should be presented by our best catechists and carried out by them with the same kind of energy and enthusiasm most RCIA teams bring to their task. We also need to approach the celebration itself as an excellent opportunity to catechize the entire community present and work with the celebrant and liturgist to plan each celebration accordingly.

Finally, we need to explore one other means already at our disposal for awakening in adults greater awareness of what it means to be disciples of Jesus. Unfortunately, it is also somewhat problematic and a mixed blessing at best. We are speaking of the current shortage of ordained priests and the impact this is having on the church. The negatives are all too obvious and will probably continue with us for some time to come. Specifically, we are speaking the growing number of priestless parishes. We are speaking of the trend in many dioceses to deal with the problem simply by closing smaller parishes and merging communities to form regional or even megaparishes in their place. Even with such adjustments, continuing to provide the eucharistic celebration and the other sacramental ministries of the ordained priesthood is becoming more and more difficult.

From the perspective of adult catechesis there is a potential positive side to the current priest shortage, however. It provides us with an excellent opportunity to explain to the people the reality and significance of their own priesthood, a priesthood to which all disciples of Jesus are "ordained" at their baptism. We can demonstrate—without diminishing the importance of the ordained priesthood—that there is very little related to the life and mission of the parish that they are not capable of doing, and in fact have the responsibility to do, by virtue of their own priesthood. We can challenge their limiting, culturally derived, and theologically inaccurate self-definition as laity and encourage them to identify themselves by the more theologically and scripturally accurate term—*priestly people*. We would be seriously remiss as catechists if we did not seize upon this providential "catechetical moment" to help foster our adults' awareness of their discipleship and priesthood to become more conscious, living, and active.

We do not mean to imply that any of this will be easy. We must still overcome the gravitational pull of 450 years of catechetical tradition that supports the academic model. Until there is a radical change in leadership, we can expect Rome to continue to be suspicious of the newfound freedom most Catholics enjoy. Rome tends to be nervous when too much emphasis is placed on the priesthood of the faithful. We can expect it will continue to try to reimpose the uniformity and centralized control over the local churches it enjoyed prior to the council. Unfortunately, this will only serve to alienate further those who have already become distanced from the church. This kind of internal tension also tends to confuse and dispirit the large middle group. Faced with competing messages—"God loves you" versus "Obey the church or else"—many adults withdraw to the edges of church life and look elsewhere to invest their time and energy. This makes it very difficult to awaken in them any enthusiasm for discipleship or the desire to invest themselves in the community of disciples.

So our task will be difficult, yes. But not impossible. Despite the obstacles, momentum for the kind of renewal we are discussing is actually growing. We already have programs and opportunities in place that can be invaluable allies in the process. We cannot expect it to happen overnight, but having finally clarified our goal we can now begin to take the first steps toward it. The rest is just a matter of time—and the work of the Spirit.

## ADULT CATECHESIS
## AND THE CATECHIZING COMMUNITY

It has long been known that when initiation into discipleship with Jesus is understood as both the goal and the process of catechesis, then the presence and vitality of a visible community of disciples is regarded as a critical element of that catechesis. Initiation and the apprenticeship it entails are by nature oriented toward full membership and participation in the life and mission of that community of disciples. Those being initiated and apprenticed need to be in an ongoing relationship with a community that is welcoming and supportive, a community that witnesses to discipleship, a community that actively mentors its apprentice disciples. Experience demonstrates, for example, that the long-term effectiveness of the RCIA process depends on the presence of such a community. Where such a community has been lacking, the idealism and enthusiasm of the newly baptized all too often turns to disillusionment and indifference to participation in the church's life.

There is a close connection between the two tasks for adult catechesis just mentioned and our efforts to renew catechesis for children and youth. They are two sides of the same coin. Whatever we do to help adults, especially parents, grow in awareness of their own discipleship will help them recognize their responsibility to foster discipleship in the children and youth. At the same time, as noted above, one of the better ways at our disposal for helping the adults grow in awareness of their own discipleship is through our efforts to establish discipleship as the goal of catechesis for their children and youth.

We need to underscore the close connection that exists between our efforts at vitalizing adult catechesis and our efforts to develop an effective apprentice program for young people. The two will tend to flow into and support each other.

## ADULT CATHOLICS AND NEW EVANGELIZATION

The *GDC* displays unusual candor for a church document in admitting that a large number of adult Catholics today are in need of evangelization. For anyone engaged in parish work, this comes as no surprise. They can go through their parish rosters and identify any number of inactive members, people one never sees except perhaps on the occasion of a wedding, the birth of child, or the death of a family member. There are those on the roster who only participate on occasion, most often on the special feast days. Also on the roster are those who dropped out for a period and then rejoined, often but not always solely out of concern for growing children. Others, though still identifying themselves as Catholic by heritage or culture, have probably been dropped from the roster because they no longer maintain any contact with or interest in the church. Young adults tend to make up the majority in this group, though all age groups are represented.

All the above groups (and others we could describe) have two things in common. First, all have been baptized into the church, usually in infancy, and never formally rejected either their relationship to Jesus or the church. Second, their relationship to Jesus and the church is no longer conscious, living, and active— and quite often never was. In short, though by virtue of their baptism they can be officially described as Christians, disciples of Jesus, and members of the Catholic Church, they still need to hear the good news proclaimed to them and they still need to be called to conversion, to discipleship with Jesus, and to active membership in the community of disciples. For want of a better term, we describe these baptized Catholics who are still in need of evangelization as *inactive Catholics* or *latent disciples*.

133

Before we continue it is necessary to make a few distinctions to ensure clarity. It is important to recall, for example, that the *GDC* uses the term "new evangelization" to describe our ministry to these inactive Catholics. It uses the term "evangelization" primarily though not exclusively to describe the ministry of proclaiming the good news of Jesus to peoples who have never been baptized. We should also note that all of us throughout our faith journey are being called to ongoing conversions, triggered by having the good news proclaimed to us (by being evangelized) in new ways or in new circumstances of life.

While *evangelization* and *new evangelization* technically speaking have different audiences, they often will be quite similar in both content and methodology. Nevertheless, it is the responsibility of catechesis and more specifically of adult catechesis to provide this *new evangelization* to our inactive Catholics. At least, the *GDC* seems to indicate that it is (see, for example, arts. 26 and 58). As such, the document has added a significant new dimension to our understanding of the nature and scope of adult catechesis. If we take the *GDC* seriously, we will need to develop a whole new branch of adult catechesis with its own special content and strategies. Implications for staffing and budget will also have to be explored.

Here we will only describe what the *GDC* identifies as some foundational principles to guide us in this new endeavor. Developing such a new branch of adult catechesis, however, is clearly a critical agenda item for the renewal of catechesis in the third millennium.

First, many of those in need of new evangelization may still carry with them a number of misconceptions, prejudices, and half-truths about the church, the truths of the faith, and about Jesus that they picked up in childhood. Many, not having associated for some time with the church, are totally unaware of the extent or true nature of the changes Vatican II has effected. They have too often formed opinions of the contemporary church based solely on the news media and popular entertainment media, neither of which is an in-depth or balanced source. Such misconceptions and half-truths are serious obstacles to hearing the good news. It is therefore important in approaching these inactive Catholics to attempt to discern if this is in fact the case and then to attempt to correct these false presumptions. For example, many, though believing in God's unconditional love, may not be aware that the church also embraces and proclaims this same conviction.

Second, as with evangelization directed to the unbaptized, new evangelization directed to inactive Catholics needs to adopt the principles of pre-evangelization and pre-catechesis. In particular we need to discern the hungers of the human spirit these inactive Catholics experience and gradually help them recognize how the good news of Jesus can answer these hungers. There are several particular hungers experienced by most contemporary adults to which the good news is especially responsive.

- Many inactive Catholics through the work of the Spirit have already arrived at the conviction that God loves them unconditionally. They consequently hunger to hear that truth officially affirmed by the church of their youth, something they have not yet heard. Thus we need to make that message the core of our new evangelization and proclaim it most enthusiastically.
- Many adults now experience society as more and more impersonal and consequently have a strong hunger for intimacy and personal relationships. The friendship and intimacy Jesus offers us through the invitation to discipleship, if properly presented, has a powerful appeal today.
- Many adults in modern society also feel a sense of rootlessness and therefore hunger for participation in community. The church in general and the local parish in particular, if properly understood and presented as a welcoming, caring, inclusive (catholic) community of disciples, can have great appeal and can also trigger an awakening of faith in our inactive Catholics.
- Many adults today are coming to realize that the material comforts and pleasures wealth can provide have no power to satisfy their deeper spiritual hungers. Also, bombarded daily in the news media with continual and often very vivid reports of ever greater human cruelty and suffering,

many are caught both in a sense of personal helplessness to make a difference and in a sense of overall hopelessness for the future of humanity and our planet. The church, on the other hand, as a community of recovering sinners and as the disciples of the risen Lord, enjoys unshakable hope for the future and the ultimate victory of God's reign. For that reason, and because of their belief in the mystery of the cross, the community of disciples proclaims that every individual's efforts to promote peace and justice, no matter how feeble and insignificant they may seem when measured against the evil present in the world, will make a difference. This message of hope and purposefulness, which is of the very essence of the good news, can have a special resonance with many of our inactive Catholics if properly presented.

By identifying the above hungers (there are other equally powerful ones), we are able to gain invaluable insight into what elements of the gospel message inactive Catholics will find most persuasive.

Applying the principles of pre-evangelization and pre-catechesis to new evangelization is only part of the task, however. A third principle is equally important. We need to discern how to shape and articulate those elements of the gospel, once recognized, in ways that will make sense to today's inactive Catholics. We are referring to the task of *inculturation,* which the GDC stresses is critical to evangelization, new evangelization, and catechesis. We need to learn how to couch the good news in language, metaphors, and images that take into account the influence of today's culture. It is a culture captivated by the apparently limitless power of science and technology. It is a culture that is increasingly more sophisticated in terms of psychology and anthropology. It is a culture that fosters skepticism and cynicism, even as it fosters naive beliefs in new religions and self-improvement movements that promise the "quick fix" for everything from weight loss to immortality. We examine inculturation in the next chapter. Here we wish only to point out that our efforts at new evangelization will usually be ineffective if we rely on the images, phrases, and "proofs" of previous times. A proclamation based on pious platitudes and the religious jargon of the past will not be heard as the *new proclamation* of the good news that the new evangelization needs to be.

We cannot hope to explore here the many practical "how to's" of the new evangelization. We are passing over, for example, the very critical question of how to create opportunities for being in contact with inactive Catholics so we can attempt to share the good news with them. To be honest, we do not have answers to many of the practical questions. Keep in mind, until the publication of the *GDC* there was no official talk of the need for a new evangelization for adult Catholics. It is a new branch of adult catechesis for the third millennium. We have the few principles just identified to guide our beginnings, but we have no models or structures in place. Discerning the hungers of inactive Catholics, developing a message that is truly inculturated, and answering those important "how to" questions are all part of the task the whole catechetical community needs to address. We need to recognize and embrace this new task as an integral part of our catechetical agenda for the third millennium.

## CONCLUSION

It is the very nature of discipleship to follow and learn from one's master. Our own discipleship with Jesus implies a permanent commitment to Jesus precisely as disciples. We are expected throughout our life to continue to learn from Jesus. We never outgrow that responsibility. That, simply stated, is the understanding we need to promote if we are to vitalize adult catechesis and make it normative for the life of the church. And that, simply stated, is the main agenda item for adult catechesis in the third millennium.

# PART II
# OTHER ISSUES RELATED TO THE RENEWAL OF CATECHESIS

## INTRODUCTION

Throughout Part I we focused primarily on that dimension of the catechetical agenda that might be considered the nuts and bolts of any catechetical program, namely, its content, structures, and methods. We attempted to describe, at least in a general way, the kind of paradigm shift that is called for in these aspects of the ministry if we are to succeed in completing the renewal of the catechesis initiated by Vatican II. In Part II we examine several other critical agenda items closely related to this renewal and its overall success. The first is the need to integrate the principles of *inculturation* into the shaping of our catechetical message and methods. The second is the need to adapt our ministry in keeping with the *signs of the times*. The third is the need for *effective catechetical leadership and advocacy* at the national, diocesan, and parish levels to ensure that catechesis is provided with the financial support and personnel it deserves as one of the church's foundational ministries. Finally, since Catholic schools have been considered one of our most vital catechetical programs during the past century, we find it necessary to explore *the role of Catholic schools in the future of the catechetical ministry*. As we did in Part I, we do not attempt to give a fully developed, step-by-step blueprint for how to proceed in pursuing these agenda items. However, we do identify most of the specific tasks involved and provide a basis for starting the process for pursuing these agenda items.

# 8

# Inculturation, Catholic Identity, and Catechesis

## INTRODUCTION

In one sense the concept of inculturation is the "new kid on the catechetical block." Though it has received a great deal of attention in recent years, that attention has been focused for the most part on evangelization. We have not yet effectively integrated it into catechesis. It has remained more or less on the fringes of our ministry and is usually spoken of only in terms of the topic of ethnic or racial pluralism.

In stressing the close connection and interweaving of evangelization and catechesis, however, the *GDC* has succeeded in bringing inculturation to the forefront as a integral and very important aspect of our catechesis. Given that it has not received adequate attention in the past and that the *GDC* stresses it, we are convinced it is a priority in the catechetical agenda for the third millennium. Integrating it effectively into our catechesis, however, will require a paradigm shift similar in scope to the shift that takes place when we reclaim discipleship as the goal of catechesis.

The nature, importance, and processes of inculturation for the ministries of evangelization and catechesis receive extensive treatment in the *GDC* (see, in particular, arts. 109–33, 203–14). Rather than simply reiterate these very instructive passages, we propose to approach the question by first reviewing certain underlying theological principles that shape our present understanding of inculturation and give direction to the catechetical processes we need to adopt. Then we examine the origins of the present concern for losing our Catholic identity that has surfaced within the catechetical ministry. We feel it can best be approached within this context of inculturation. Finally, we attempt to apply the principles of inculturation to catechesis to see what changes it will require in how we are to do our catechesis in the third millennium.

In the process we need to examine inculturation within the church's history in order to understand the practical implications as well as the challenges involved in the task of reintegrating it into catechesis in our day.

## UNDERLYING THEOLOGICAL PRINCIPLES

An example may help us to identify the principles at work in inculturation. Suppose we were to gather a group of people, each with a special artistic talent: a poet, a musician, a painter, a sculptor, a mime, a choreographer, a playwright. We give all of them the same basic assignment: express the concept of freedom in your particular art form. We assume that all are in basic agreement about the meaning of the word *freedom* and that each is able to do the task successfully.

Each of the completed works can now stand alone as an authentic expression of the concept of freedom. Yet when viewed together in all their diversity we have a much fuller appreciation of the meaning of freedom and perhaps discover nuances of the concept, previously unperceived.

The artists, for their part, will discover as they proceed with the task that certain aspects or elements of their particular art form lend themselves quite easily to the expression of freedom. Others cannot be used as readily or even stand in opposition to the concept.

Inculturation of the gospel is much like that. Each culture is like a particular artist. If asked to express the vision and values of Jesus and discipleship with Jesus in its own "medium," each culture will produce a work that can stand alone as an authentic expression of that gospel. Yet when we view the work of the various cultures

142

together, we all gain a much fuller appreciation for the meaning contained in the gospel and discipleship, and we discover nuances and insights previously hidden to us.

The incarnational principle is therefore *the* underlying theological principle of inculturation. The Word of God becomes flesh. The Word becomes spoken in the form and within the limits of the created universe. This is possible because, as Karl Rahner so profoundly describes it, the created universe in general and humanity in particular by its very nature has an affinity for God, a capacity to receive, give expression to, and ultimately be transformed by God's Word.

Thus, the particular expression given to the word of God spoken to Abraham and through him to all his descendants was "incarnated," was shaped and formed and expressed through the medium of their culture and continued to be reshaped and reformed and re-expressed as that culture evolved over the centuries. Ultimately and most fully the word of God is spoken to all of us in the person of Jesus. The Word of God didn't become flesh in some abstract sense, however. The Word of God became a first-century Jew.

Inculturation is essentially the continuation of that process. Though the Word of God became a Jew, the first disciples, who were themselves Jewish, were sent to proclaim Jesus to all nations and all cultures. Each nation, each culture, each new generation to which Jesus is proclaimed is called to give its own unique expression to the Word once received, to incarnate Jesus' vision and values in keeping with the gifts and limitations proper to it. So the incarnational principle implies a process analogous to a dialogue, the kind of praxis we spoke of in the previous chapter. Just as those who are open to the word allow themselves to be enlightened and reshaped and transformed by it, so the word allows itself to be shaped, expressed, or incarnated in new ways.

A second important theological principle of inculturation suggested by our example of the artists is that God's word has been present and active in all cultures even before the gospel is formally proclaimed to them. The essence of any culture is the core convictions and values it uses to shape its political and economic structures, to determine its ethical norms, and to guide its social interactions. Just as our artists discover that certain core elements of their particular medium lend themselves quite readily to the expression of freedom, so God's word has already sown in each culture the seeds of certain convictions and values very much in harmony with the gospel. This principle plays a critical role in both evangelization and catechesis. If we can discern the convictions and values a people already possess that are in harmony with the gospel, we have an excellent entry point for our ministry and for initiating dialogue with them.

This second principle leads in turn to a third principle. Just as our artists discover that certain elements of their medium do not lend themselves to the expression of freedom, so we can expect to find in all cultures certain elements, certain convictions and values and consequent behaviors and ethical norms, that are in opposition to rather than in harmony with the gospel. Just as we seek to discern what in a given culture is already in harmony with the gospel and can be used to give it new expression, so we need to discern and then challenge and guide people to reject those expressions that are obstacles to the gospel's authentic expression.

We can identify a fourth principle contained in our example. No one art form can fully capture and express the concept of freedom, nor can it be considered the *best* medium for doing so. In the same way, no one cultural expression can fully incarnate the word, nor can any one culture be considered the *best* for doing so. However, just as a review of the various art forms taken together provides a more comprehensive understanding of freedom's many facets, so the incarnation of the gospel in all its possible diverse cultural forms will give us a much more comprehensive understanding of the mystery of Jesus and what it means to live as his disciples.

There is a fifth theological principle at work in inculturation that is very important. We presumed that there is one underlying and unchanging meaning to the term *freedom* to which the artists agreed and which they sought to express through their various art forms. In the same way we are presuming there is one underlying and unchanging meaning contained in the Word, God speaking to us in Jesus, even though it can be expressed authentically in various forms. An example may help here. Suppose that the standard way Rome executed its criminals and political rebels at the time of Jesus had been death by hanging. Suppose that this is how Jesus was executed. Try to imagine the radical change that would have had on how we express our faith. The central symbol of our faith could well be a gallows or perhaps a noose. That change would have had profound ripple effects in the composition of our hymns, devotional life, the official prayers we use in liturgical rites, art, and even the architecture of our churches. Yet, and this is the critical point, all of the actual meaning contained in the mystery of Jesus' death would remain intact. The noose rather than the cross would now be a symbol of God's mercy, Jesus' obedience and trust in the Father, and our redemption. Our own call as disciples to be willing to "put our head in the noose" would contain the same meaning we now give to expressions like "taking up our cross."

Granted, so ingrained is the symbol of the cross that even to talk this way can seem irreverent. But it does illustrate that what is most critical in the process of inculturation is that the underlying meaning contained in God's revelation to us in Jesus be authentically preserved, maintained, and proclaimed. That is the primary criteria to use in judging if any particular cultural expression of our faith is valid.

We need to identify one final theological principle of inculturation, even though it is not contained in our example above. Certain symbols of our faith, although having their origins in a particular culture and period of history, now possess a universal quality and can be considered essential to the expression of our faith in all cultures. The cross, as just seen, is one of them. Jesus did in fact die on a cross, not on a gallows. The cross is and will remain, therefore, our best and official symbol for expressing the meaning revealed in the death of Jesus, and it should be used in all cultures. Having said that, each culture does has some freedom in expressing that universal symbol. Thus we have the Celtic cross, the Greek cross, the Germanic cross. The eucharistic meal is another universal and official symbol, the essence of which needs to be maintained in all cultures. Music, gestures, and other elements reflecting a particular culture can be incorporated into its celebration, but it must remain in essence the sacrificial meal inaugurated by Jesus at the Last Supper (which in turn has roots in the Jewish Passover meal).

## AN INHERENT THEOLOGICAL TENSION

The latter two principles reveal an inherent tension that exists when we attempt to take inculturation seriously. On the one hand, we need carefully to preserve and maintain the revelation given to us in Jesus. On the other hand, we must remain continually open to the need to give it new expression and allow it to be incarnated anew by each culture that receives it.

Because the church was born and in its earliest days existed entirely within the first-century Jewish culture, it did not initially experience that tension. The risen Jesus was proclaimed from within, as it were, as the messiah that had been promised to the Jewish people. We find an example of that primordial proclamation in Peter's address to the people recorded in Acts 2. Peter quite easily drew upon the scripture and the history of the Jewish people in making his point, being a Jew himself. In the same way the early church adopted and adapted rituals already rooted in the Jewish culture, such as baptism and anointing, when it sought to celebrate and symbolize a person's conversion and birth to new life in Jesus. In a real sense the church in Jerusalem remained Jewish. Its members continued to go the Temple and to observe various Jewish dietary laws. Inculturation as such was not an issue.

It quickly became a tension-filled issue, however, when Paul began to preach not just to the Diaspora Jews but to the Gentiles. Suddenly the church was confronted with questions: Are circumcision and the Jewish dietary laws essential elements of the good news revealed in Jesus? Are they to be preserved and maintained in each new culture as essential elements of discipleship with Jesus and fellowship with the community of disciples?

When the church came to grips with this issue at the Council of Jerusalem (Acts 15), both what was decided and how it was decided had profound significance. First, they had the courage and wisdom to let go of certain time-honored religious traditions, traditions that were "in their bones," as it were, and had served them well. They came to realize that, as good as these were, they were not essential to discipleship with Jesus. In fact, they might serve as obstacles to authentic discipleship in other cultures. Second, they arrived at this decision in a communal manner and through dialogue. It was viewed as the task of the community as a whole acting through its recognized leaders, not individuals acting independently, to determine what is essential to discipleship and what is not.

What is truly remarkable is how little the church actually required of converts after that council (see Acts 15:23–29). In this first experience of the need for inculturation in proclaiming the good news, the early church gave great freedom to its new converts to give expression to their discipleship in keeping with their own culture.

The Gentile church comprised largely persons immersed in the culture of the existing Roman Empire. As the Jerusalem church was able to adopt and adapt various Jewish customs and rituals quite easily, the Gentile church exhibited a similar wisdom. For example, the celebration of the birth of Jesus, the Light of the World, eventually came to coincide with and borrow various features from existing pagan feasts such as the Saturnalia. This pagan feast was celebrated about the time of the winter solstice and was a feast of lights with which the new Christians were very familiar. This inculturation had its false starts, of course. For example, Paul quickly found out that the Greek tradition of *agape* did not mix well with the Lord's Supper, and he had to step in and establish some rules in order to maintain and preserve the authenticity of the Eucharist.

Once the church came out of the catacombs into the mainstream of society, the process of inculturation grew apace. For example, the churches built so the community could assemble in public were often modeled after existing public buildings of assembly, the basilicas. Theologians began to use the idiom and principles of the dominant philosophical systems of the day to explain the good news.

This effort is reflected very clearly in the creedal statements and doctrinal formulas the church developed at its great councils in the fourth, fifth, and sixth centuries. The community adapted much of the existing imperial government's organizational structures, such as dioceses, to its own structures. In short, much of the church's history in those early centuries was the history of a continuing process of inculturation. And this process continued to a large extent as the church first began to attempt to bring the gospel to the barbarian tribes at the fringes of the empire and beyond.

While much of this history is quite familiar, we have sometimes failed to notice the freedom and ease with which the church in those early days applied what we now recognize as the principles of inculturation. It seems to have been a virtually instinctive process. Yet at some point, difficult to pinpoint with any historical accuracy, inculturation ceased to play this vital role in the church's missionary and catechetical ministry. It is as if what had been the church's living tradition became frozen in time. The experience of the Reformation solidified this attitude. The church began to impose on new converts, regardless of their particular culture, the religious traditions, spirituality, ritual practices, and doctrinal formulas that it had developed through the processes of inculturation in an earlier time and in a different culture. In the same vein, its missionaries began to impose various convictions and values of the current European culture from which they came onto new converts. We are now painfully aware of the harm this missionary mentality too often wrecked upon indigenous populations, for example in the New World in the sixteenth and seventeenth centuries and in sub-Saharan Africa in the nineteenth and early twentieth centuries.

Though we cannot pinpoint exactly when the church ceased to feel free to apply the principles of inculturation to its evangelization and catechesis, we do know that Vatican II has laid the ground work for restoring inculturation as integral to both these ministries. In fact, the fundamental questions the council asked had their roots in the principles of inculturation: How can the church today articulate and incarnate the vision and values of Jesus within a society radically different from the Jewish and Greco-Roman cultures in which the church originated? What must be preserved and maintained as essential to discipleship with Jesus and what can and should be let go? As noted before, it is precisely because of these questions that Karl Rahner compared the work of Vatican II to the Council of Jerusalem and considered it to be the second truly great revolution in the entire history of Christianity.

Not surprisingly, the tension inherent in the task of inculturation came to the fore almost immediately after the council, and we continue to experience it to this day. Though we oversimplify, this tension is the source of the current concern for Catholic identity and the fear that since Vatican II this identity is in danger of being lost. This concern can be expressed in the form of the question: In our rush to renew the church, are we failing to maintain and preserve essential elements of what its means to be disciples of Jesus and members of the community of disciples established by him?

The council fathers were well aware of their responsibility to maintain and preserve the essential elements of the revelation we have received in Jesus, of what is essential to discipleship and to the nature and mission of the community of disciples he established. At the same time, they showed great courage and wisdom in recognizing that certain customs and practices, ritual forms and institutional structures acquired over the centuries, good as they may have been for their time and culture, were not essential. They also admitted that various doctrinal formulas, reflecting the idiom, scientific knowledge, and philosophical constructs of previous ages, do not adequately communicate their underlying meaning and truth to people in our day, whose idiom, scientific knowledge, and philosophical constructs are often quite different.

It is important to note that the underlying meaning contained in all our essential doctrines was never a question in the council's deliberations: the triune nature of God and God's act of creation *ex nihilo;* belief in the divinity of Christ and the belief that he is also fully human; our redemption through Jesus; the validity and value of the sacraments; the primacy of the Eucharist in our sacramental system and its nature as the sacramental re-presentation of Jesus' sacrifice on the cross; the nature

149

and role of scripture as God's word; the communion of saints; the unique role Mary plays in salvation history; and so forth. It simply asked, sometimes explicitly, sometimes by implication, if we need to give new expression to these mysteries in doctrinal formulas, liturgical rituals, moral code, and in the way we organize and live out our lives as the visible community of the disciples of Jesus.

Needless to say, virtually everyone, hierarchy and people alike, was caught off guard by the nature of the council's work. The church's members had been effectively conditioned for over four hundred years (probably much longer) to believe that all our doctrinal formulas, liturgical rituals, devotional practices, and the laws that governed our behavior were unchangeable and beyond question. While some quickly got caught up in the spirit of the council and welcomed the fresh air that rushed in through the "opened window," others were and have continued to be alarmed, concerned that we are in the process of losing our Catholic identity.

Since the council never challenged the underlying meaning of essential doctrines, we need to ask what the council *has* challenged that some continue to perceive as also essential and how this is viewed as a threat to what they consider our authentic Catholic identity. Recognizing the elements the council suggested we can and perhaps should discard if we are successfully to evangelize and catechize people in today's cultures is at the very heart of our overall quest in this chapter, namely, to determine how best to integrate and employ the principles of inculturation into our catechesis in the third millennium. Let us review these elements along with the issues they raise.


## INCULTURATION ISSUES RAISED BY VATICAN II

We focus here only on the issues that seem to most disturb those who fear we are losing our Catholic identity. These issues include the following, which we present as statements, each of which we will then examine briefly:

- Being Roman or Western European is not essential to authentic discipleship or to the life of the community of disciples.
- Being hierarchical is not essential to discipleship or to the organization of the community of disciples.
- Being patriarchal is not essential to discipleship or to the organization of the community of disciples.
- Being the one true church does not preclude the possibility that other Christian churches and other religions also possess truth revealed by God and can be instruments through which people can gain access to redemption in Christ.
- Exegesis is an invaluable and often essential aid in our quest to discern and rearticulate for today's cultures the underlying meaning of the truths revealed to us in the scriptures and defined in our tradition's creeds and doctrinal formulas.

The statements are our own, but their sense can be found, sometimes explicitly and sometimes by implication, in the council's documents. It should be obvious why these conclusions of the council can be regarded as dangerous threats to certain time-honored presumptions about what is essential to Catholic identity. Some of these statements can be especially disturbing because they challenge elements that seem to be in the very bones of the church, having been present or assimilated at its very origins. So let us examine the validity of each statement in turn.

## Being Roman or Western European Is Not Essential to Authentic Discipleship or to the Life of the Community of Disciples

Strictly speaking, discipleship with Jesus, which is at the core of Catholic identity, is not by nature Roman or by extension Western or European. Whether by divine providence or historical circumstance, the visible community of disciples of Jesus began its existence within the geographical and cultural context of the Roman Empire and did eventually center itself in Rome. The influence of that civilization remains with the visible organization of the church and its customs and practices to this day. We cannot

151

understand the church's history apart from that influence. Yet, it remains true that there is nothing *inherently* Roman about discipleship or the community of disciples. By extension there is nothing *inherently* European or Western about the visible church either. It would not lose its authentic identity if it chose to make Swahili its official language rather than Latin. It would not lose its authentic identity if it chose to recodify its laws using something other than the ancient Roman legal model. Nor is authentic discipleship distorted if a church building in Japan were to be built to look more like a Shinto temple than a European cathedral.

That the community of disciples is not inherently Roman or Western was stressed over and over by the participating bishops at the Asiatic synod held in 1998. It is understandable that the European missionaries who so heroically sought to spread the gospel to the Americas, Asia, and Africa from the sixteenth through the nineteenth centuries brought with them the characteristics the visible church had acquired from having been immersed for fifteen centuries in Western European culture. But as the Asiatic bishops pointed out so emphatically, many of these Roman and Western characteristics can be obstacles to the successful proclamation of the gospel in Asia today. They tend to impede rather than promote the development of an authentic discipleship in these Asiatic countries.

The underlying point here is that if we are to promote authentic discipleship in today's cultures we will have to move beyond our Roman and Western European origins. This does not mean we need to abandon wholesale all those Roman or Western European characteristics the community of disciples has acquired over the centuries. Some continue to serve us well, are in harmony with the basic gospel message, and have the capacity to transcend history and specific cultures. For example, the liturgical year, though rooted in the Western calendar and in seasonal rhythms of the European climate, maintains a certain universal quality that can translate into all cultures and climates with appropriate adaptations.

We now need to make a few comments about the official title *Roman Catholic*. The *Roman* part of the title is a historically acquired description that, while useful, is not of itself integral to the definition of the community of disciples established by Jesus. *Roman,* as it is used today, has two levels of meaning. It is used, on the one hand, to distinguish various segments of the church ritually; it refers to those communities within the universal church that celebrate their sacraments according to the Roman rite rather than, for example, the Greek or Coptic rite. The term *Roman* is also used to identity those Christians who regard the bishop of Rome to be the authentic successor of Peter and the official leader of the universal church. There are others, however, who consider themselves Catholic (as opposed to Protestant or Reformed) who do not regard the bishop of Rome in this way, such as the Anglican Catholics, and the Greek and Russian Orthodox Catholics.

The term *Catholic* began to be used as a title rather than as a descriptive quality or mark of the church in response to sixteenth-century reformers such as Luther. It was used to identify those who rejected the proposed reforms of Luther and the other "protesters," accepted the leadership of the pope as the successor of Peter, and embraced the teachings of the Council of Trent as the authentic or orthodox expression of church's beliefs from the time of the apostles onward. It is in this way that *Catholic* continues to be used today, distinguishing this Christian community (which we are calling *the* church) from other Christian communities, such as the Lutheran, Methodist, or Baptist churches. Thus the title *Roman Catholic* continues to be useful as a distinguishing and descriptive title, but of itself it sheds no real light on the church's authentic identity.

In fact, the term *Catholic* is in some ways an unfortunate choice. When first introduced to describe a quality or mark of the community of the disciples of Jesus, *catholic,* as its Greek root implies, referred to a certain universal quality the community possesses, an unrestricted openness, the capacity to embrace and incorporate all truth and all peoples, a community where distinctions like *Jew and Gentile, slave and free, male and female* had no meaning. By extension, it suggests the qualities of inclusivity, receptiveness, and hospitality. In this light the use of the word *Catholic* as a narrowing or restricting term, or to separate one Christian community from others, is something of an oxymoron.

It might have been better during the time of the Reformation had the church fathers used a term like *Petrine church* or perhaps *Apostolic church* rather than *Catholic* Church to distinguish itself from those churches that they considered were breaking from the Petrine or apostolic tradition.

It is obviously impossible today to effect such a name change. In both religious and secular spheres the title *Roman Catholic* is too deeply embedded, and we can expect that it will continue to be used. But it is good to be reminded that the term *catholic* in its original sense identifies the quality of openness and the capacity to embrace and incorporate all truth and all people as being essential to the true nature of the community of disciples established by Jesus. And it is good to be reminded that the title *Roman* goes against the true meaning of the community of disciples' *catholic* nature when used as a kind of indictment upon those "not *Roman*."

## Being Hierarchical Is Not Essential to Discipleship or to the Organization of the Community of Disciples

Other qualities the community of disciples acquired that are not integral to its true identity relate to how it has organized itself politically. (We are not using the word *political* in any pejorative sense here, but simply as the normal need and process of visible human communities to organize and give order to themselves.) Presently the church is organized *hierarchically*. It also maintains certain elements of the *patriarchal* model. Both of these are acquired characteristics that are not inherent to its nature. They have been borrowed from the cultures and civilizations in which the church found itself, first in its beginnings and later during the Middle Ages in Europe. *Hierarchical,* as used here, describes a political system, a way of organizing society by ascribing certain rights and responsibilities to its citizens in a descending order from king or lord through a noble class and downward to peasants and, in some cases, to slaves and "untouchables." *Hierarchy* also has other meanings besides this political one. It can be used as a model for organizing reality theologically, philosophically, or scientifically; for example, we can speak of a hierarchy of truths and values from the most important to the least important, or a hierarchy of animals and plants from the most biologically complex to the simplest. Thus we can talk about the church possessing a hierarchy of truths, and we may find it useful to describe in hierarchical terms the charisms it possesses without being obliged to say that as a visible community it has to be politically structured as a hierarchy.

As a political system the *hierarchical model* has been widely used throughout history. On the positive side, it has proven to be an effective way to organize large groups of uneducated and undisciplined people, maintain order, and direct people's energies toward certain common goals. On the negative side, it can be turned into an oppressive form of government, holding the people in a state of ignorance and servitude. The church, as it gradually over time adopted this hierarchical model of governance, has enjoyed its various advantages and also experienced some of its negative effects. As a political system, history shows that whenever the common people become more educated (as in Europe after the invention of the printing press), the hierarchical or monarchical form of political system no longer functions well. The rights and privileges of the ruling classes begin to be challenged, often by force, and some more democratic or egalitarian form of political system tends to evolve (as was the case in Europe from the eighteenth century onward). It is similar for the church. As the laity have become better educated, they have been expressing greater dissatisfaction with the hierarchical model of church governance.

We need to point out that by saying the church's hierarchical political structure is not inherent to its nature and identity, we are not implying that the church is inherently democratic either. We use the term *democratic* here to describe a specific political system of "one person, one vote" and majority rule. To demand that the church organize itself politically as a democratic society actually has no more validity than demanding that it organize itself hierarchically. The fact is, in terms of political structures the church is neither inherently hierarchical or democratic, so neither of these political systems should be considered integral to its nature. At Vatican II the council fathers, having recognized this, began to reclaim and outline the elements of a more communal political model that is more true to the inherent nature of the church, one guided by the principles of collegiality, subsidiarity, dialogue, and consensus.

## Being Patriarchal Is Not Essential to Discipleship or to the Organization of the Community of Disciples

*Patriarchy* as a model can be either social or political or both. Basically, it is a model that ascribes to males either within the family and society or within a political system the roles of authority and leadership. Within a patriarchy women may (or may not) be treated with respect, protected, and cared for with great solicitude, but they remain socially and/or politically subservient to males. In terms of the church, the patriarchal model was adopted early on from the societies and cultures wherein it originated. Though it served more as a social model originally— "Wives, be subject to your husbands"—it eventually became intertwined with the hierarchical political model, with women assigned lower places within the hierarchy and being virtually excluded from any role of leadership or decision-making in the political sphere. The influence the patriarchal model had on women's roles within the church is further complicated by the influence the ideal of celibacy began to exercise over the church.

Much recent scholarship, especially the work of feminist theologians, has revealed the inherent flaws of the patriarchal model. It has been used to justify and perpetuate the domination and oppression of women throughout history in the political, economic, social, and religious spheres. As such, it contradicts the gospel, and there is nothing about the inherent nature of the church that says it must use patriarchy either as a social or as a political model to remain true to its authentic Catholic identity. In fact, as we enter the third millennium one of our greatest challenges continues to be to extricate these historic elements of patriarchy from the church's self-understanding and institutional structures and lay claim to the model our feminist theologians have persuasively demonstrated is more in harmony with true nature of the church, namely, a partnership of equals.

*Being the One True Church Does Not Preclude the Possibility That Other Christian Churches and Other Religions Also Possess Truth Revealed by God and Can Be Instruments Through Which People Can Gain Access to Redemption in Christ*

Since the church had spent the previous four hundred years defending itself against the challenges of the various Christian churches that emerged after the Reformation, the above insight is perhaps the most revolutionary and most courageous one arrived at by the council. For that reason it is also one of the most disturbing for those who fear the church is losing its authentic identity. For one thing, it opened the door for Catholic involvement in the ecumenical movement. Though progress in this movement has been uneven and has suffered its share of setbacks, it continues to move forward.

This insight also has led us to reexamine the nature of the church's relationship to the reign of God, toward which all creation is ultimately oriented. By happy (or unhappy) circumstance the early church "grew up" within the most advanced and powerful civilization of its day. In turn, the church itself became a major civilizing agent, first as it confronted and went out to the various barbarian hordes and then in its role as the keeper of the flame of civilization when the Roman Empire began to disintegrate in Western Europe. This civilizing role of the church became more and more entwined with the emerging feudal (and hierarchical) political system. This, in turn, culminated in the establishment of the Holy Roman Empire, in which the church and society in all its sociological, cultural, political, and economic dimensions became virtually one and the same.

This joining of the church, the body politic, and society predictably had a powerful influence on the church's popular self-understanding. The reign of God proclaimed by Jesus and the temporal reign of the church came to be understood as one and the same. As a result, other civilizations and cultures, not just other religions, came to be viewed as inferior to the church and inadequate for salvation. A variety of popular attitudes within the church were translated into theological principles. For example, the idea that the pope held ultimate temporal authority over all the earthly kings and other political rulers became such a principle. A certain theological triumphalism developed, leading to misinterpretations of the church's role as mediator of the universal salvation won by Jesus. The concept that "outside the church there is no salvation" was popularly understood by leadership and laity alike to mean that salvation depended upon membership and allegiance to the visible church. This concept, especially when joined with European colonialism, had a very harmful effect on both the motives and methods of its missionaries.

Vestiges of regarding the church and the reign of God as coterminous remain embedded in the minds of many Roman Catholics even today, and they consider this an integral aspect of Catholic identity. Thus we can understand why they find it disturbing to suggest that God's revelation also may be present in other Christian churches and other world religions, and that these also may have a role to play in establishing the reign of God. Or why they find it disturbing to suggest that the church can and should work in partnership with these other churches in establishing God's reign. Or that they find it disturbing to suggest that the church can possibly learn from these other religious traditions.

Yet, awareness that no one culture or system of thought can ever fully incarnate God's word goes to the very heart of inculturation. It does not deny that *the* church, the community of disciples of Jesus that traces its roots back to Peter and the apostles, possesses the fullness of God's revelation and has a unique role to play as a sacrament and sign of the presence and promise of God's reign. But it admits that the community of disciples will be able to better understand the revelation it has received through dialogue with other religious traditions as they attempt to incarnate God's word as they have experienced it. In the same way the church will be a more effective instrument for the establishment of God's reign by cooperating with rather than competing with or trying to "conquer" these other religious traditions.

*Exegesis Is an Invaluable and Often Essential Aid in Our Quest to Discern and Rearticulate for Today's Cultures the Underlying Meaning of the Truths Revealed to Us in the Scriptures and Defined in Our Tradition's Creeds and Doctrinal Formulas*

The Council makes it clear that a fundamentalist or literalist mentality can only be an obstacle to our attempt to evangelize and catechize effectively today. That is, we cannot hope to communicate the gospel and the mysteries contained in the revelation we have received in Jesus by simply bringing forward previous articulations of this word that were born and shaped in previous cultures. The council has no argument with the truth contained in these previous articulations. It is simply maintaining that the underlying meaning or unchanging truth they do contain needs to be discerned and then rearticulated (reincarnated) in and for today's cultures.

Most mainstream Catholics today recognize that biblical exegesis has helped us better understand and gain new insights into the scriptures. By studying the cultures in which the various books were written and how these cultures affected their development and articulation, we have been able to gain new insights into the purpose and meaning intended by the original authors and by later redactors. Consequently, we are better able to understand the meaning these scriptures should have for us today.

Applying the same principles of exegesis to the development of our creed and doctrinal formulas is much more problematic for those who feel that such statements are so foundational to our faith as to be "written in stone." To tamper with them through exegesis is unthinkable, a direct threat to the faith itself. Thus, to venture beyond the Aristotelian constructs of substance and accident, nature and person, for example, in an attempt to describe the mystery of the Trinity, the incarnation, or Jesus' real presence in the Eucharist in ways more understandable to people today is to corrupt the faith. To introduce the concepts of the Big Bang, the evolution of the solar system, or the evolution of life on our planet into our doctrinal statements regarding creation *ex nihilo* endangers our belief in God as Creator.

The fact remains, however, that this is precisely the kind of task required if we are to take inculturation seriously. We must at the same time raise a legitimate caution. Both scriptural and doctrinal exegesis demand a high degree of scholarship and training in a wide range of academic sciences, such as ancient languages and the laws of linguistics, cultural anthropology, history, archeology, sociology. Unless we ourselves are trained theologians or scripture scholars who are well schooled in such sciences, we catechists must be willing to take our lead from those who are. Those who oppose the kind of exegesis suggested by the council are definitely correct in saying we are dealing with the very foundations of our faith. So the task can never be taken lightly. We must approach it with humility, and we must apply our very best scholarship to it.

Inculturation means, among other things, that we are free and that we must be willing to let go of certain nonessential characteristics of our faith acquired over the centuries in order to make the underlying meaning of the gospel and discipleship understandable to people today. We have discussed some of these nonessential characteristics that Vatican II either explicitly or implicitly identified as necessary to move away from if we are to effectively proclaim the gospel in the modern world.

We have attempted to demonstrate that much of the concern expressed over the loss of Catholic identity, especially as this applies to catechesis, has its roots in a failure to understand or to accept the principles of inculturation that guided and motivated the council. The concern arises from the inherent tension that is present whenever we attempt to discern what needs to be maintained and preserved and what can be abandoned.

We can expect continued resistance to our catechetical efforts to pursue inculturation in keeping with the directives of Vatican II, and more recently, the *GDC*. Nevertheless, we should not be discouraged. Nor can we allow this sincere though misguided concern for Catholic identity to impede us from carrying out the necessary tasks involved in inculturation. Let us now examine in more detail how inculturation influences catechesis.

## INCULTURATION: ITS APPLICATION TO CATECHESIS

Though the actual process is much more complex, inculturation basically directs us to answer this simple question: How can we best communicate to *these* people in *this* culture what it means to be disciples of Jesus and a community of disciples? To integrate inculturation into our catechesis in the third millennium and to answer the question it asks, we suggest certain guidelines.

### We Have to Approach Catechesis from a Missionary Perspective

Much of the early literature dealing with inculturation focuses on evangelization. The principles of inculturation were initially applied primarily to doing missionary work in non-European, non-Christian cultures. The need for inculturation is more or less self-evident in those situations, a point stressed quite clearly by the 1998 synod of Asian bishops.

However, we sometimes tend to forget that an underlying motivation of Vatican II was to make the gospel understandable to the entire modern world. The council fathers understood that the culture of the Western world and the so-called Christian countries is also to some extent "foreign" and non-Christian. This modern culture is radically different from the cultures that shaped the church and its faith expression for the past nineteen hundred years. In the council's view the principles of inculturation need to be applied to *all* cultures, not only "foreign" missionary work.

This fact was not missed by the *GDC*. It stressed not only the close theological and pastoral connection that exists between evangelization and catechesis but also that in today's world, including the Western societies that have long been aware of and influenced by Christianity, catechesis will often demand a new evangelization. It will need to employ some of the same strategies, including inculturation, that we have previously reserved only for missionary work in non-Christian, non-Western cultures. So even though our primary focus here is on the renewal of catechesis in the United States, we will to a certain extent need to view and apply the principles of inculturation in much the same way as a missionary might when going to a foreign land.

## *We Need to Take Seriously the Pluralism of the Cultures That Exist in the United States*

The idea of pluralism is certainly not new to catechesis. It has been an ongoing concern for several decades now. However, to a large extent we have tended to define pluralism primarily in terms of ethnic minorities, and the ministry's concern has focused primarily on the need to develop catechetical materials that better reflect the cultures of those minorities. Though there has been some success in this regard, it has proven to be a much bigger challenge than at first imagined.

For the most part, our catechesis during the years since Vatican II has continued to employ an academic model. For example, we have periodically attempted to develop national tests. We have sought (in vain) to develop a nationally uniform curriculum. We try to develop scope and sequence charts. Periodically some of the bishops consider the possibility of a nationally uniform textbook series.

During the same time the number of publishers of catechetical materials has shrunk significantly. Though each of the publishers that remains has its own way to package its programs (and each is quite good), the programs themselves are essentially the same. The arrival of the CCC and the establishment of the U.S. Bishops' Office for the Catechism are now adding to this trend toward homogenizing catechetical materials.

While this quest for uniformity makes sense in terms of our present academic approach to catechesis, it totally ignores the urgent need for inculturation. It ignores the reality that American society is now a *bona fide* missionary territory. It also ignores the reality that our society has many subcultures in addition to the more obvious ethnic minorities.

Youth have long been recognized as such a subculture, and to their credit many youth ministers have instinctively recognized the need to apply principles of inculturation in their attempts to catechize them. Generation X is another subculture. Though catechists have certainly begun to address this group, we also need to take much more seriously the significant cultural differences that exist between rural and urban people. And there are significant differences regionally; the Eastern seaboard, the Midwest, the South, the Northwest, Southern California, and others have their own characteristics.

Granted, there is a shared or commonly experienced national culture. But it is still safe to say that materials and methods that "work" when catechizing in one of the boroughs of New York will probably not "work" as well in the Mississippi Delta or rural Montana. We have already discovered that translating a textbook series from English to Spanish and adding photos and art work reflecting Hispanic culture is not inculturation. In the same way it is virtually impossible to devise a catechetical program (textbooks, lesson plans, and so forth) that will work equally well in all parts of the country.

The authors of the CCC clearly recognized the need to develop national and regional catechisms. The GDC stressed the same point. Thus we should strive to reverse the trend toward the homogenization of catechetical materials. We are called upon to develop not just a national catechism but also regional and even diocesan catechisms, all shaped by the principles of inculturation. In place of national textbook series we should begin to develop apprentice manuals for discipleship for the various regional, ethnic, and age-group subcultures, guided by these more specialized and inculturated catechisms.

It is perhaps becoming more clear why we said earlier that catechesis will experience a paradigm shift if we begin to take inculturation seriously. Both catechists and the publishers of catechetical materials will face a tremendous challenge. On the positive side, if we redefine the goal of catechesis in terms of discipleship and extricate catechesis from the academic model, the task becomes more manageable. Discipleship by its nature is open to diverse cultural expressions or incarnations. When discipleship is the primary goal, rather than a set of truths about discipleship, there is no need for a uniform curriculum to maintain unity among diverse cultural expressions. Unity from one cultural expression to another is primarily maintained through the common source of our discipleship, Jesus. Also, the small-group and praxis model we are proposing by nature allows participants to bring their own (culturally shaped) experience into dialogue with the gospel and to incarnate it in keeping with that experience.

Recognizing and responding to the many diverse subcultures in our country is going to be quite challenging, even if we should succeed in redefining the goal and extricating catechesis from the academic model. We believe, however, that if we fail to take seriously the pluralism of cultures in our society and fail to make the suggested paradigm shift in our catechetical goal and structures, inculturation will remain more of a buzz word than a reality in our ministry.

*The Inculturation of Our Catechesis in the Various*
*Subcultures Will Require That Our Catechists Be*
*Immersed in Those Cultures and That They Be Given*
*Both Local Autonomy and Freedom of Expression*

Inculturation must take place *from within* the particular culture. Today's missionaries attempt to follow this principle. They now recognize the error of missionaries during the colonial period in Europe. They realize the importance of attempting to immerse themselves within the culture they hope to evangelize. Only by experiencing the gospel from within the culture can they begin to understand how to express it in metaphors that are rooted in the experience of that culture.

The author of Matthew's gospel was so effective in writing to his community of Jewish converts because he was himself Jewish. Luke's gospel spoke effectively to its Gentile audience because its author was a Gentile convert. Both were writing from within their respective cultures. It must be noted that each also experienced a sense of freedom and used a degree of literary license in shaping the essential gospel story he had received to meet the needs of his intended audience.

It is much the same today. Effective local catechists are already within the culture they are seeking to catechize and can thus "speak the language" of the local community. Ideally, we should be able to say this of each local bishop as the chief catechist of each diocese. Obviously, Hispanic DREs have a significant edge on Anglos, no matter how fluent their Spanish, when it comes to the inculturation of catechesis for the Hispanic community. In the same way, experience demonstrates that the most effective youth ministers tend to be quite young themselves and are still familiar with the culture of the teens they hope to catechize. Likewise, the most effective DREs tend to be those who grew up in the area where they now minister. It is important to note that it took the emergence of women theologians writing from within their own feminine experience to give us totally new insights into the meaning contained in the gospel, freed of the encrustation it has received from the male-dominated patriarchal cultures through which it has passed for almost two thousand years.

Such "local catechists" who are already immersed in the culture or subculture they seek to catechize also need to be granted a degree of autonomy and a freedom analogous to literary license in developing their programs. This is true whether "local catechists" means a bishop's committee developing a regional catechism to be used for catechesis in Appalachia; a group of catechists helping a diocesan office develop catechetical programs for a diocese in central Kansas; a local DRE developing a program for his or her inner-city parish, which serves a particular ethnic minority; or a catechetical team developing a program for its large, midwestern, suburban parish, which serves a predominately white, middle-class membership.

While outright censorship may be too strong a description for it, the present trend in the church in the United States is toward exerting greater centralized control and requiring greater uniformity in the development of catechetical programs and materials. Concepts like local autonomy, freedom, and literary license are not looked upon kindly in such an atmosphere. To promote such concepts in our catechetical ministry understandably evokes in some ecclesial authorities fears of a kind of "creeping congregationalism" at best and sheer theological and catechetical anarchy at worst.

Yet it is the official documents of the church that advocate the need for more local autonomy and freedom to develop new expressions of the gospel that reflect the cultural pluralism of the United States. We can trace this official teaching from the documents of Vatican II through the *GCD* and *Catechesi Tradendae* and most recently in the *GDC*.

There is no way we could hope to predict when the apparent contradiction between words and deeds, between head and heart, between official church teachings and official church practice will be resolved. It is understandable that it is difficult for the official church to accept a degree of local autonomy and an increasing pluralism in the expression of the faith after experiencing over four centuries of rigid uniformity of expression shaped by only one dominate cultural experience—an experience interpreted almost exclusively by white, male theologians of Western European descent who were also ordained, celibate clergy. We can be sympathetic and perhaps even patient. Yet until we are willing to grant a degree of local and autonomy and freedom to catechists and until we come to accept pluralism of expression as normal for the faith, inculturation will have only a superficial impact on catechesis and there will be no authentic renewal of catechesis in the third millennium.

*Inculturation Must Take Place in Dialogue with Qualified Scholars, the Larger Community of Faith, and the Magisterium*

This principle at first glance may seem to cancel out the previous one. Properly understood, this is not the case. First, the freedom analogous to literary license that we spoke of is not to be equated with total lack of restriction. As catechists we must be not only open but eager to have others in the larger faith community, including the church's official teachers, evaluate our efforts at inculturation. We have the same responsibility as all disciples to preserve and maintain the essential revelation we have received in Jesus.

We need the objective view of other qualified persons to help us answer this basic question: Is the *fundamental meaning* of the gospel adequately preserved in the particular expression we are giving to it in our local situation? Not being willing to seek help in answering this question will always be irresponsible.

Also, we must not attempt to venture beyond our competence when it comes to scriptural and doctrinal exegesis. In these areas especially we need to stay abreast of the latest scholarship and to be open to seeking advice from experts as necessary.

But note that critique and evaluation need to be carried out in a *spirit of dialogue.* We must trust the competence and expertise of those to whom we go for advice. They, in turn, must trust us. They must recognize that our motives are rooted in the principles of inculturation, principles with which the evaluators must already be familiar and comfortable. They must respect our competence as catechists and the our expertise in relation to our particular culture.

It may be premature to talk of such dialogue taking place. In fact, it is a moot point until such time as church authorities, including the magisterium, begin to accept the need for local autonomy and freedom contained in its own teaching on inculturation. Nevertheless, when the time does come and we are granted a degree of local autonomy and freedom in doing catechesis, we will also have to accept the responsibility to seek the advice and counsel of the larger faith community.

## CONCLUSION

Integrating the principles of inculturation into catechesis involves a shift in our perspective in a number of areas. We will need to adopt a more missionary attitude. We will have to recognize and become more comfortable with the diversity of cultures and subcultures present in our country and with the diversity of catechetical programs needed to serve them. We will have to be willing to let go of certain time-honored presumptions about the faith.

As with the other catechetical agenda items we have been discussing, this one also calls for experimentation, collaboration, and cooperation within the catechetical community. As yet we have no answers to the practical question of how to go about inculturation in our ministry. Nevertheless, if we are to complete the goal of renewing catechesis begun at Vatican II, we have to include inculturation as an essential item in our catechetical agenda in the third millennium.

# 9

# Catechesis and the Signs
# of the Times

## INTRODUCTION

A dominant theme of Vatican II was the church's responsibility to discern the initiatives of the Spirit being revealed to it through certain *signs of the times*. The council stressed the importance of aligning the church's message and mission with these actions of the Spirit in contemporary society. There is a close connection, of course, between the effort to discern the Spirit's presence in a particular culture's enduring core values and this effort to discern the Spirit's action in certain contemporary movements and events that are exercising a major influence on society at large. Therefore, there is much similarity between the catechetical task of inculturation and the catechetical task of reading the signs of the times.

As with much of what Vatican II promoted, the idea of asking the church to ally itself with certain new movements in society went against a long-standing tradition the church had acquired. Regarding itself as having already been entrusted with the fullness of God's revealed truth, it had long been very suspicious of all new ideas and movements arising in secular society. This defensive and suspicious tradition rose almost to the level of dogma during the pontificate of Pius IX, who led the church against what he called the dangers of Modernism.

The church has at times been overly suspicious of new ideas. Still, when we in the catechetical ministry first embraced the concept of reading the signs of the times as an important task, we were not always adequately discerning. Too often we uncritically adopted ideas and trends into our message and methods that have since proven to be only fads. It is to be hoped that we have learned from those naive and potentially harmful mistakes and can now approach the task of reading the signs of the time with more wisdom and circumspection. In any event it remains a major item on our catechetical agenda for the third millennium. The Spirit is definitely active in our society today, patiently yet powerfully prodding and guiding humanity toward the destiny God intends for us. It is essential that we accurately discern these movements of the Spirit and align our catechetical message and methods with them.

Here we can only sketch out some of the more obvious signs of the times that call for further discernment. They are easily recognized because, whether we like it or not, they reflect major shifts in how we understand ourselves and our world. Those which do prove to reveal initiatives of the Spirit will need to be integrated into our ministry if we hope to be effective in the third millennium.

## THE SHIFT TOWARD GLOBAL INTERDEPENDENCE

It has often been pointed out that the famous first photograph of Earth taken by astronauts, which showed it as the isolated, limited, and self-contained planet that it is, had a powerful effect on our collective psyche. We began to talk of Spaceship Earth. It began to dawn on us that we really do need to learn how to live together and also how to preserve the limited resources we have if the human race is to survive on this very finite planet.

This new awareness of humanity's interdependence, which is continuing to emerge and take shape, is reflected in a whole series of movements. Each is in its own way a radical new view that challenges age-old presumptions about ourselves and our relationships to one another and to our planet. We describe some of these movements briefly here.

*Ecological Interdependence*

Though it continues to be an uphill battle, there is now a powerful movement afoot to reverse the present worldwide practices of pillaging and polluting Earth's limited resources and to shift to practices of conserving them. The biggest, though not the sole obstacle, is the consumerism that dominates the lifestyle of the developed countries and consequently drives their economic and industrial policies. For the environmental movement to be successful—and the future of our world ultimately depends on it—the developed countries will have to experience a conversion that leads to the adoption of a radically different, less selfish, more responsible lifestyle, one that takes into account the long-term well-being of *all* peoples throughout the world. Assuming this movement is of the Spirit, it seems imperative that we adjust our catechetical message accordingly by calling today's disciples to support and become involved in this movement to conserve and sustain Earth's resources and to reject the consumerism that is endangering them so they will be available to future generations.

*Political and Economic Interdependence*

Just as our growing awareness of interdependence is awakening in us the need to reevaluate how we are to use Earth's limited resources, it is calling us to reevaluate the political and economic systems that control how we distribute those limited resources. It is becoming clear that the nationalism and colonialism of the Western world, which dominated world politics for nearly five hundred years, is no longer a viable system. Nor is unbridled capitalism an adequate economic system, because it is driven solely by the profit motive and depends upon constantly expanding markets created by increasing consumerism. Both are "dinosaurs," though current headlines often seem to contradict that premise.

Granted, nationalistic, religious, and ethnic wars between age-old enemies seem to be multiplying rather than diminishing, and the gap between rich and poor nations seems to be widening rather than narrowing. But we are now beginning to recognize that neither

171

situation is normal or tenable. Although we seem a long way from establishing the international political and economic structures that can eliminate the political violence and economic inequity, there is growing awareness and increased efforts at all levels of society and in all areas of the world of the need to do so.

The church's continuing work to promote peace and justice and the efforts of an ever-increasing number of secular groups and organizations to foster political and economic reform at the national and international levels are both inspired by the same Spirit. It seems imperative, then, that our catechetical message in the third millennium foster awareness of the disciple's responsibility to promote peace and justice precisely by supporting and becoming involved in those secular movements that are committed to the same goal.

## Cultural Interdependence

Through the advances and pervasiveness of communication technology, we are literally wired together today as one people. We have now become that "global village" first described by Marshall McCluhan back in the 1960s. Communication technology has made possible an unprecedented exchange of ideas and intermingling of cultures. In the long term the potential for growth in mutual understanding and mutual respect is unlimited and can provide the essential interpersonal foundation for growth toward becoming a true world community. All cultures can be enriched in the process.

An unfortunate but predictable short-term effect is the spawning of radical and often militant fundamentalism—both religious and ethnic—in those who feel their security and/or identity is being threatened by this intermingling of cultures. This unfortunate but understandable reaction can also be found within the church. There are always dangers, of course, such as the kind of religious pansyncretism that developed in the later stages of the Roman Empire. Besides the risk of an uncritical religious relativism, we also face the danger of a bland homogenization or leveling of cultures to the lowest common denominator. The worldwide popularity enjoyed by jeans, Coke, and rock music is one such example of this phenomenon.

Despite these risks the newfound ability of private citizens and whole nations to communicate with those of different cultures and continents promises to be a great ally in fostering the kind of understanding needed if we are to learn to share and to support life on this planet. It seems safe to say that the movement toward unity is being inspired by the Holy Spirit. It also seems safe to say our own catechetical message needs to promote rather than warn against growth in communication among all peoples if it hopes to be truly *catholic* in the third millennium.

## Global Interdependence: A Summary

Those familiar with the writings of Pierre Teilhard de Chardin will recognize his vision for the future unfolding with uncanny accuracy in these shifts away from individualism toward interdependence and ultimately toward the simplicity and unity of what he calls the "Omega Point." Even more important, the awakening of humanity's awareness of its interdependence and of its need for cooperation for survival is now the context in which the message of Jesus is being proclaimed. As long as it had been considered necessary, normal, and honorable for various peoples to live in isolation and/or to compete with one another for political and economic control of Earth's resources by means of violence and oppression, the Christian message was viewed as a nice religious ideal but not as something to be taken seriously in "the real world." Now, however, the "real world" faces self-destruction unless all peoples learn to live together as one family, governed by global principles of political justice and the equitable distribution of this world's resources. The world is finally acquiring the "ears to hear" the gospel precisely as the universal and authentic good news for which it has always hungered.

This growing awareness of our global interdependence is perhaps the single most dominant sign of our times. Precisely because it is effecting a paradigm shift that undermines most of the political, economic, cultural, and even religious presumptions out of which most of the world's societies have operated for so long, we can expect strong resistance to this movement for some time to come. But, assuming it is the work of the Spirit, it will prevail. It is critical that we promote and support this growing awareness through our catechesis. We will find that it is a catechetical message that resonates with the message the Spirit is actively planting in the hearts and minds of the human community in our day.

## THE FEMINIST MOVEMENT

We use the term *feminist movement,* though admittedly inadequate, to describe a variety of different movements that taken together are having the effect of finally establishing women as equal partners with men in the human project. Anthropologists observe that the presumption that the male is superior to the female and therefore has the right to dominate the female in all aspects of life had its origins in the simple fact that the male is physically stronger than the female. This ability to dominate and control the female physically eventually led to institutionalized dominance and control in all aspects of society—domestic, political, cultural, and religious. This institutionalized male dominance was established in virtually every society in some form or other, most often by the adoption of the patriarchal model. It led to the universal presumption of overall male superiority and until recent times went almost totally unchallenged. That this presumption of male superiority with all its ramifications is now being effectively challenged is one of the most important signs of our time, one that is generating a paradigm shift that will affect every aspect of human society.

Clearly, the struggle to effect this shift is far from over. It continues to meet with strong resistance, often in very subtle but effective economic and political policies, in the developed countries. In less developed countries it is just being introduced, often at great peril to the women and men courageous enough to challenge the deeply entrenched tradition of male dominance. Various world religions, including the Catholic Church, offer some of the greatest resistance to the feminist movement because they have made male dominance an integral part of their belief systems and institutional structures. The presumption of male superiority and the consequent right of males to dominate females have been so pervasively supported in theology, literature, history, and political and domestic structures that many, both men and women, find it difficult if not impossible to imagine any other way of organizing society.

Yet, the movement continues to gain momentum. In the process it is leading us to reevaluate the false presumptions of innate superiority in all their forms (racial, economic, ethnic, religious) and the patterns of institutionalized dominance and oppression they have established over those considered inferior. This, in turn, is leading us to question the presumed right of those who consider themselves superior to use force and violence to maintain and extend their institutionalized dominance and control.

Thus, in attempting to claim their own equality with men, at least some women have also become the champions of all oppressed peoples, male and female, and strong advocates for nonviolence and against institutionalized use of force in any form. When understood in this light, does not this feminist movement in all its ramifications harmonize perfectly with the message of Jesus and his vision of God's reign, an inclusive, caring community of equals living together in justice and peace? We think it is safe to presume that the feminist movement is of the Spirit. It has the potential to be the single most revolutionary and redemptive movement in our time. For that reason we consider it a sign of the times, a sign with which we need to align the catechetical message as quickly as possible.

## THE TECHNOLOGICAL AND SCIENTIFIC REVOLUTION

Advances in science and technology seem to be growing exponentially each year with no end in sight. On the surface we experience these advances primarily in terms of the new gadgets and conveniences technology is making available for our homes, automobiles, and work places. We are awed by the ever-increasing power and accuracy of the military weapons and machines science and technology are able to provide. We have developed a blind faith that medical science will eventually cure all the physical and emotional ills that beset us. We have come to trust that technology will ultimately solve all the shortages in natural resources we are beginning to experience and the problems of pollution that our lifestyle has generated.

But whether we look to astrophysics or subatomic physics, to biology, chemistry, computer technology, or the medical sciences, there is one common denominator that has the characteristics of a true sign of the times. All these advances are forcing us to set aside virtually all of our previous assumptions about who we are and what our place in the universe is. In the light of the power of the modern computer, what is human intelligence? Considering our increasing power to begin a human life in a petri dish, determine the baby's sex and other characteristics, what is the human person? In view of the recent discoveries in astronomy regarding the origin, age, and vastness of the universe with its millions of galaxies and countless billions of stars like our sun, we are being forced to ask if we are truly alone in it.

Having to ask who we are is forcing us to reexamine all our philosophical and religious assumptions. It is a critical sign of the times that we are now being forced to redefine ourselves as human beings. The presence and sheer weight of the scientific data we continue to accumulate make it imperative that we bring our faith into dialogue with science. This is not the time to retreat to the false security of religious fundamentalism. Truth is our ally, and that includes scientific truth. Therefore, in response to this sign of the times we must trust that our understanding of the fundamental convictions of our faith will be enriched and not threatened by that dialogue. If it is true that our theological convictions can be clarified and deepened by new scientific knowledge, it is equally true that society's growing scientific knowledge needs to be enlightened and informed by those same faith convictions entrusted to us.

Often lacking the light the gospel can shed on new scientific knowledge, our society today is showing signs of being very vulnerable. As it loses confidence in the old "answers" that provided it with self-understanding and the security of absolutes, our society is beginning to hunger for new absolutes upon which to anchor its self-understanding. Because many people, especially the young, are prone to be unreflective and uncritical, and because they have grown accustomed to expecting a "quick fix," they are now in danger of turning to the growing number of false prophets who are all too eager to pander to their hungers and their fears. The popularity of the New Age movement (usually old superstitions presented in slick new packages), the attraction of fundamentalist religious with their simplistic "black and white" answers, the rise of numerous cults and sects with charismatic leaders and promises of escape from the doom to come—all are symptomatic of a society cut loose from the traditional moorings that had provided a sense of identity, security, and direction. It is in such a society that we are now called to catechize.

As catechists we need to maintain a careful balance. Science and technology are neither gods offering salvation from all our ills nor demons determined to destroy us. But, unenlightened by the gospel, science and technology easily can be mistaken for either. We must shape our catechetical message so the next generation of disciples is able to see science and technology that way, as potential allies in the process of building the kingdom. This will be no easy task, but it is only when we succeed in placing science and technology in dialogue with the gospel that their true potential for good will be realized.

## A Satellite Society

One particular child of our scientific and technological revolution deserves special attention as a sign of the times, namely, the Internet. We alluded to it indirectly above when speaking of the communication that is now possible among all peoples of the world and the consequent potential to grow in our understanding of ourselves precisely as a global community. Like all science and technology, the Internet is neither savior nor demon. It is a tool. Like all tools, it has the potential to be used for good or for ill. It is too early to say which way the Internet will be used. But because of the growing availability of this specific form of communication, it deserves special attention by catechists.

The basic question for us as catechists, of course, is how we might put this tool at the service of the gospel as a means for more effective catechesis. There are no easy answers here, and we must be cautious not to repeat our previous mistakes and turn it into some kind of catechetical fad. For one thing, the very nature of the communication it provides is problematic for us as catechists. It provides a vehicle for impersonal or anonymous communication. As such, it can isolate and insulate its users from authentic interpersonal relationships. Given the fact that faith itself and the nature of the faith community is in essence rooted in interpersonal relationships, what are we to make of Internet communication?

Granted, this impersonal and anonymous communication can in the right circumstances lead to authentic interpersonal communication. Also, as some have pointed out, e-mail and chat-room relationships are not too different from having pen pals, except that the exchange of letters is now much faster. And, as experience indicates, this electronic tool can be a wonderful and inexpensive way to stay in touch with people with whom one already has a personal relationship.

The Internet can also make an almost limitless amount of information and number of services available to people without leaving their desk. Its potential as a tool for distance learning, especially when coupled with the use of satellite TV, is truly exciting. Alcoholics Anonymous uses chat rooms on the Internet to conduct AA meetings "attended" by thousands each day. Because such processes eliminate face-to-face contact, something is no doubt lost, but this must be balanced against the potential good that can be achieved by electronic learning and communicating.

So, for good or ill (probably for both), electronic communication in its various forms is becoming an integral part of contemporary society and as such will be an integral part of the life of future disciples as well. Learning how to use it well and also learning to avoid its potential harmful effects are critical elements in our catechetical agenda for the third millennium. Some catechists have already begun to address these issues, of course. But it will take a concerted effort by the entire catechetical community to discern what is truly of the Spirit in this sign of the times and to learn how to align our ministry with that movement of the Spirit.

## CONCLUSION

The above review of the signs of the times is admittedly limited and selective. Other significant movements could be identified. Within the church the continuing priest shortage is certainly one. So are the emerging voices of the Asian and African churches. In society there is the "graying of the population" as the baby boomers grow older. The continuing movement toward greater ecumenism can be regarded as a sign of the time that resonates with the growing awareness of overall interdependence.

Those we did treat, albeit briefly, we chose because, on the one hand, they are some of the most obvious, and on the other hand, because they seem to have the most potential to effect authentic shifts in how we will understand ourselves and how we will structure our society in the future. In indicating that we think they are of the Spirit, we do not mean to imply that no further discernment is needed before we attempt to align our catechetical message and methods with them. A wholesale and uncritical embrace of any of these movements can bring the danger of excesses, distortions, and a new dogmatism every bit as harmful as the dogmatism it replaces. This is the risk any time there is a shift in society, and we need to be careful to avoid falling into that trap.

This much is clear, however. If our catechesis is to be effective in the third millennium, we need to address these signs of the time, using all the collective wisdom we have at our disposal. It would be a serious mistake if we ignored them as if they were not affecting us and continued to go about our ministry in a "business as usual" manner. It would be just as serious a mistake to label them dangerous and harmful innovations to be opposed. As Vatican II urged us and the *GDC* reiterated to us, we need to give them our full attention in an attempt to discern where the Spirit is leading us and how we can adapt our ministry and its message to ensure that we cooperate with the movements of the Spirit.

# 10

# The Catechetical Agenda
# and the Role of
# Catechetical Leadership

## INTRODUCTION

There are actually two tiers to catechetical leadership. The first tier is represented by the bishops who serve ex officio as our chief catechists. The bishops exercise this leadership is three basic ways. First, they have the responsibility to oversee and maintain the orthodoxy of the message being proclaimed in their respective dioceses. Second, through initiating and/or endorsing the development of various official catechetical documents, such as *To Teach As Jesus Did* and *Sharing the Light of Faith,* they fulfill their responsibility to clarify the nature of the ministry and give it a general direction. Third, they have the responsibility to establish the overall structures and provide adequate resources of personnel and finances to carry out the ministry in their dioceses. By extension, parish pastors function in this first tier of leadership because they are considered ex officio the chief catechists in their respective parishes with duties rather similar to those of the bishop in whose name they serve.

The second tier of leadership consists of those delegated by the bishops and pastors to do the "hands on" work of implementing the ministry, namely, the directors and staffs in charge of the overall diocesan catechetical programs and, by extension, the DREs in charge of the local parish programs. Our focus in this chapter is on this second tier of leadership and the role it is to play in carrying out our catechetical agenda for the third millennium.

As we see it, this second tier of leadership has two basic tasks:

1. To advocate on behalf of the catechetical community so that catechesis regains its rightful place and is provided the necessary resources as one of the church's essential ministries.
2. To help the catechetical community form a consensus concerning the overall goal of the ministry, the specific priorities to be pursued at this point in time, and the strategies for pursuing them.

We hope to outline, at least in general terms, the steps needed to address these two tasks.

## A GLANCE TO THE PAST

A brief review of how the second tier of leadership was organized and functioned in the late 1960s and through the 1970s can be instructive, because it was very effective. As some will recall, in those days the nation's diocesan directors were organized as the National Conference of Diocesan Directors (of Religious Education) (NCDD). The conference operated under the auspices of the bishops as an official department of the United States Catholic Conference of Bishops (USCCB).

The NCDD had several characteristics that made it very effective in those days. As a group that was both endorsed and financed by the bishops, it enjoyed the confidence of the bishops, who looked to it regularly for direction and advice in fulfilling their ex officio catechetical leadership. In short, it had the credentials that allowed diocesan directors to maintain an effective dialogue with the bishops and to advocate for catechetical ministry at both the national level and within their respective dioceses.

The NCDD was also a relatively small group, under two hundred members, made up almost entirely of diocesan priests.

This gave the group members a certain natural camaraderie and cohesiveness and also enabled them to deliberate in a more or less personal manner. This, in turn, allowed for efficient deliberations and relative ease in the development of consensus—though often only after some stimulating and colorful debate. Thus the group developed a unified view of the priorities to be pursued based on and in response to the insights of Vatican II and the catechetical scholarship that followed in its wake. Though we are oversimplifying here, in general terms these priorities were developed around three key insights that the group sought to promote nationally among the catechetical community:

1. Faith is relational, not just cognitive.
2. Methodology needs to become more experiential and to include the new insights in educational theory.
3. Both our content and our methods have to become more age appropriate, reflecting the new insights of psychology regarding stages of intellectual and emotional development.

We do not mean to imply that this was a utopian period for catechesis, but during this period the NCDD did provide excellent national leadership for catechesis. It was able to influence the bishops and to promote in the dioceses a unified national thrust to the ministry. Unfortunately, the NCDD's ability to provide effective national leadership began to deteriorate quite rapidly in the 1980s.

## A PERIOD OF DECLINE

Perhaps the most significant cause for the decline in the NCDD's ability to provide the much needed national leadership just described was the fact that the bishops ceased endorsing it as an official catechetical department in the USCCB. In efforts to reorganize for reasons of economy, the bishops chose to drop the NCDD and several other related departments from the organizational structure of the USCCB. NCDD thus lost its official status as a national body of catechetical leadership. Individual diocesan directors could no longer approach their respective bishops with the weight of an official national body behind them.

Because the NCDD had lost the prestige of being an official department in USCCB, a number of diocesan directors no longer thought maintaining membership was important and dropped out. As a result the conference found itself fighting for survival and began to direct much of its energy to maintaining its own existence. This further eroded its ability to exercise national leadership and provide a sense of direction for catechesis at the national level.

About the same time (whether there is a causal relationship is uncertain), we entered a period during which the catechetical ministry splintered into various "special interest" groups, each competing to some degree for the attention and support of the catechetical community. There was the RCIA movement, for example, and the youth ministry movement, each of which developed its own national organization. We had advocates for the family-centered movement and the lectionary movement. Adult education maintained its own separate organization, and the catechetical leaders of the Hispanic community formed their own organization to address their own special needs. DREs began to organize at the diocesan and province level to pursue their own professional interests. Grassroots organizations formed to promote alternative models for catechesis. Each of these efforts, of course, had legitimacy, but a period of confusion and lack of national consensus ensued that remains to this day.

In the midst of this splintering several other trends further eroded the unity and cohesiveness of the catechetical community. Sometimes for budgetary reasons and sometimes in response to growing complaints regarding the effectiveness of our catechesis, some bishops and pastors began to cut funding and consequently personnel for catechetical ministry. Simultaneously, we began to experience a "vocation shortage" in qualified catechetical personnel. As the old guard retired or moved to other ministries, it became more and more difficult to attract a new generation willing to pursue a career in catechetical ministry. Finally, the catechetical community now finds it necessary to compete for funds and personnel at both the diocesan and parish levels with new ministries that have come on the scene during the much noted "ministry explosion" that has taken place within the church in recent years.

## LOOKING AHEAD

Though we have painted a rather dire picture of the present catechetical scene, one apparently devoid of national leadership, there are several indications that we have turned the corner, as it were, and are poised to enter a new era of effective leadership and national consensus. The first reason for this optimism is the providential advent of the *GDC*. As an official document endorsed by Rome and drawing upon the authority of all the major catechetical documents that went before it, the bishops can be expected to give it serious consideration. Since it clearly proclaims the central role catechesis needs to play in the church's mission, it can prove a great ally to the second tier of leadership in its task of advocating on behalf of catechesis today.

In much the same way, by identifying and promoting discipleship as the overall goal and organizing principle for catechesis it provides today's leadership with a unifying theme around which to unite and focus the energies of the various and sometimes competing groups that now make up the catechetical community.

Finally, the shape the National Conference of Catechetical Leadership (NCCL) has taken in the process of evolving out of the former NCDD is equally providential. At its core remain the diocesan directors and their staffs. But it has expanded to embrace by direct membership, affiliate membership, or through networking virtually every segment of the catechetical community: diocesan and provincial DRE organizations, the RCIA forum, the Hispanic catechetical leadership, the national youth ministry, adult education organizations, the Eastern churches, theologians, publishers of catechetical materials, those in leadership in behalf of catechetical ministry to the physically or cognitively challenged, and experts in media and electronics.

The journey to reach this point has not been an easy one. Though the NCCL has continued to exercise some valuable national leadership in recent years through pursuing various important projects, such as the development of the national DRE standards and the *Echoes of Faith* catechist training program, much of its energy in recent years has been directed toward achieving its reorganization. It is to be hoped that the NCCL is now in position to assume the mantle of national leadership on behalf of the catechetical community that was once exercised by its forerunner, the NCDD. For that to take place, however, it seems imperative that it now begin to aggressively take certain steps.

## NCCL: THE CHALLENGES IT FACES

We do not presume to tell the NCCL what it must do, of course. Neither can we provide it with a step-by-step process for achieving the goals we are recommending. We make these recommendations out of respect for its membership and out of the strong conviction that of the various catechetical organizations that presently exist, none is better equipped to provide the national leadership that is now needed.

We believe the tasks, as stated in general terms above, are these:

1. To advocate on behalf of the catechetical community so that catechesis regains its rightful place and is provided the necessary resources as one of the church's essential ministries.
2. To help the catechetical community form a consensus concerning the overall goal of the ministry, the specific priorities to be pursued at this point in time, and the strategies for pursuing them.

We have also already indicated that the *GDC* can be an invaluable ally in both tasks. The church's leadership can be expected to be attentive to an appeal by the NCCL to give greater attention and priority to the catechetical ministry when the credibility of their advocacy is founded upon the identical message proclaimed in the *GDC*. The document's advocacy for discipleship as the central goal of all forms of catechesis provides an equally creditable and compelling basis for uniting all segments of the catechetical ministry around a single unifying theme and priority, while allowing each to pursue its own special aspect of the ministry in a way proper to itself.

Describing the tasks is one thing. Actually carrying them out, even with the support provided by the *GDC,* is clearly another. In the 1990s various interest groups within the catechetical community have often felt it was necessary to "protect their own turf" in order to survive. This has sometimes led to a kind of ideological entrenchment by various groups around certain "schools of thought" regarding appropriate priorities and the best ways to proceed with the catechetical agenda. In short, the catechetical community remains to a large degree a house divided.

It would seem that the NCCL, having embraced through membership or networks of communication with virtually all the various catechetical groups, needs to continue to gain the confidence of these groups. It needs to assure them that it is motivated not by the concern to protect or expand its own "turf" but only by the desire to advocate effectively on behalf of the entire catechetical community. In the process it will have to convince these groups—if they should need convincing—that it is to their mutual benefit to form and present a united front in their dialogue with the bishops, regardless of the group they choose to officially represent them. History has shown that working in isolation none of them, including the NCCL, has been able to gain sufficient credibility to persuade church leaders to reverse the continuing trend toward downsizing the catechetical ministry in all its forms at the diocesan levels. And without a clear signal from the bishops, most pastors do not feel any need to reverse the trend in parishes either.

Let us assume that the NCCL can form a consensus among the various catechetical groups, enabling them speak with one voice.

There remains the actual task of dialoguing with the bishops on behalf of the ministry, advocating that they take the necessary actions required to restore catechesis to its proper status within the church's mission, the status that all the catechetical documents claim for it. Again, we are not prepared to suggest how the NCCL might best initiate and structure such a dialogue. It is at the very least a politically delicate task that, if mishandled, could end up evoking the ill will and suspicion of the bishops rather than their support and encouragement. At the same time it is a task that must be pursued. This is not a time for timidity. The very future of the catechetical community for at least a generation to come depends in no small part on fostering such a dialogue now. If the NCCL should choose not to accept the challenge to act—and as quickly as feasible, we might add—it runs the risk of losing all credibility as the catechetical leadership conference its name implies and could well become one more well-intentioned but ineffectual support group for aging diocesan leaders and their diminished staffs.

## DIALOGUE, CONSENSUS, AND THE CATECHETICAL AGENDA

Should the NCCL achieve the task of becoming the vehicle for reestablishing authentic unity and collaboration among the various catechetical groups, its task of fostering a common vision among them around the theme of discipleship should, at least in theory, be relatively easy. The *GDC* provides the necessary documentation. It is basically a matter of encouraging and facilitating dialogue within the catechetical community around the core message in the document. Possibilities for such dialogue include the sponsorship of a national catechetical convention, regional meetings, and study weeks for the leadership that represents each of the groups, to name a few. In any event it is critical that one group take the initiative in sponsoring this kind of dialogue, and the logical group for the task is the NCCL.

What needs to emerge from this dialogue, in addition to a consensus regarding the overall goal of discipleship as presented in the *GDC*, is the specific catechetical agenda for the third millennium and agreed-upon strategies for pursuing that agenda. For example, it will take coordination and collaboration among the various catechetical groups to effect the shift to the goal of discipleship fostered by a relational model and away from cognitive goals fostered by an academic model. Numerous questions have to be resolved by this dialogue, such as:

- How will we develop the needed discipleship apprentice model? How will we determine the appropriate insights, values, and skills of discipleship to be introduced into the apprenticeship at the various ages of the children and youth and their particular stages of development? What support materials will be needed by the apprentice disciples and by the catechists? Who is to be responsible for developing them? How can various possible models of apprenticeship best be tested and evaluated?
- Who is to take the initiative in showing catechists how to apply the principles of inculturation contained in the *GDC* so they will know how to inculturate their message and apprentice program in order to ensure that it will be couched in the metaphors, images, and formats most appropriate to the groups to whom they minister? How can these principles and their practical implications best be communicated to catechists?
- How are we to work together to discern the signs of the times? Once discerned, how do go about incorporating their implications into our catechesis?

Though we have identified the above as critical agenda items for the third millennium, the catechetical community may choose to identify and give higher priority to others. But it will not be enough to name the agenda through the dialogue we recommend that the NCCL initiate. There also must be eventual agreement on responsibilities and strategies for carrying out various elements cooperatively. Though we have suggested that NCCL is perhaps best suited to initiate the dialogue itself, all segments or groups in the catechetical community will need to participate and share responsibility for carrying out the agenda agreed upon, each in keeping with its own special focus and expertise.

## THE ROLE OF DREs

Effective advocacy for catechesis at the national level and a collaborative agreement by the various catechetical groups regarding our common goal and specific agenda for the ministry involves the DREs as an integral part of the second tier of leadership in several ways. First, a number of DRE organizations already have a voice in the process through their membership in the NCCL. Their involvement in the NCCL gives them the opportunity and the responsibility to exercise significant national leadership on behalf of catechesis.

Second, we can expect the diocesan staffs who are participating in the NCCL to work closely with DREs in their respective dioceses, helping them advocate for the ministry at the parish level in dialogue with pastors. We can also expect diocesan staffs to solicit the support and involvement of the DREs in the process of adopting the goal of discipleship, developing appropriate apprentice models, and implementing the various other items of the catechetical agenda contained in the *GDC*. As experience proves, it is here at the grassroots that catechetical renewal proposed by the document must ultimately be effected or it will remain, like so many documents before it, just another book on a shelf in our offices and archives.

Third, DRE organizations, both diocesan and provincial, need to recognize that they have both the right and the responsibility to exercise leadership on their own. They can take the initiative, if necessary, to establish dialogue with their diocesan staffs, with their bishop, with national leadership organizations like the NCCL. Given their grassroots perspective, DRE organizations are in an ideal position to recognize what needs to be done to renew catechesis in local areas. At the same time, the NCCL has given them the structure and capability to network with diocesan and provincial DRE organizations throughout the country. Thus they have tremendous potential to exercise leadership if they choose to speak out with a unified voice. They should begin to speak out together and to offer their insights and support—and when necessary their criticism—in order to help formulate and implement the catechetical agenda for the third millennium.

## DRE LEADERSHIP CRISIS?

To many, the above description of the leadership role of DREs and their untapped potential for exercising it at a diocesan and national level may seem unrealistic. They can point out that we are now experiencing a serious shortage in professional DREs. Many parishes still willing to offer adequate compensation to attract qualified DREs cannot find them. Some parishes, because of budget cuts or a shift in priorities, are unwilling even to seek professional DREs. For these and other reasons, an increasing number of DRE positions are now being filled by well-intentioned, often part-time "amateurs" recruited from among the core of local volunteer catechists. Though possibly still maintaining the title of DRE, many in this new wave of parish catechetical leaders lack the time, interest, or financial support required to participate in their diocesan DRE organization. So how can we realistically expect DRE organizations to fulfill the leadership role we ascribed to them?

To address this legitimate question we need to examine the issue in its proper context. First, most DRE organizations, despite the attrition in membership they have experienced of late, continue to maintain both the numbers and the ministerial competency needed to carry out such a leadership role. Second, there is a direct correlation between the lack of availability of competent DREs and the lowering of status catechesis has experienced at both the diocesan and parish levels. If we can succeed in reclaiming the kind of status for catechesis called for by the *GDC*—which should be one of our most pressing agenda items—it is safe to predict that we will at the same time once again be able to attract competent people to the ministry.

Third, we also need to remember that the very nature of the DRE's "job description" will change radically if we succeed in reclaiming discipleship as the proper goal of catechesis and identify the more relational model of apprenticeship as the proper means for achieving it. To date, because we remain entrapped in the academic model, the job description of the DRE continues to resemble that of a professional educator more than a catechetical minister. We may be pleasantly surprised to discover that many of those "unqualified" DREs now directing parish programs do possess the charisms needed to be very effective catechetical leaders once they are no longer required to provide an essentially academic program. We may need only to provide support and some additional formation for them.

Granted, there are quite a few "ifs" in the scenario we just presented. The fact remains that we have every reason to be optimistic. Even in their diminished state most diocesan and provincial DRE organizations possess the numbers and expertise to participate as leaders in effecting the needed changes both in the status of the ministry and in how it is defined and carried out in the future. If they are willing to exercise that leadership role within and on behalf of the larger catechetical community, they will at the same time be playing a major role in resolving the DRE shortage and in redefining the nature of that ministry within the church.

## CONCLUSION

Some may think what we have been outlining is too idealistic or too naive. But the *GDC* does exist, and the NCCL now has in place the organizational structures to provide this kind of leadership. The catechetical community is hungering for a new vision and will be receptive to dynamic leadership that can breathe new life into the ministry that presently tends to be floundering rather aimlessly in maintenance mode. Our DRE organizations possess tremendous untapped potential.

In short, what we are proposing is based on a realistic appraisal of our strengths as a catechetical community. Though the tasks outlined are by no means simple, they are achievable if the NCCL and the various other leadership groups within the catechetical community set aside their differences and work together. If we do not act now, using the momentum the *GDC* is providing, it could be another generation or more before we have another opportunity to complete the renewal of catechesis begun with Vatican II.

# 11

# Catholic Schools
# and the Catechetical Agenda

## INTRODUCTION

Historically, the Catholic schools in the United States can be considered one of the great success stories of the American Catholic Church. They were born out of the desire to protect and hand down the faith to our children in a society perceived as hostile to the church. They were established and maintained through the remarkable generosity of the laity, most of whom were working-class people, and the total dedication of the countless women and men religious who staffed them. The faith and vitality of the United States church today can be traced in no small part to the school's effectiveness as instruments for preserving and handing on the faith. However, much has changed both within the church and within society over the past 150 years. We therefore need to review the nature of the schools' relationship to the church's overall catechetical ministry and ask what role they are to play in the third millennium. We examine these issues briefly here.

## SOME TENSIONS

When the schools were first established, their nature and purpose were clear. They were perceived as a necessary tool for the very survival of the church in the United States. Today their nature and purpose, and consequently the question of their necessity, are more problematic. The current preoccupation with the

194

need to define and reclaim the Catholic identity of our schools, including those of higher education, is symptomatic of their problematic status.

We can illustrate the uncertainty we now experience regarding our schools by listing a series of questions that are now being frequently asked:

1. Has the need to achieve and maintain academic excellence, a prerequisite if the schools are to maintain adequate enrollment, distracted attention from their essentially religious mission?

2. Having lost the services of virtually all the women and men religious who had formerly operated them, can they maintain their religious character, their Catholic identity, while being staffed primarily by laity?

3. Do they too often continue to reflect an ecclesiology of isolation and defensiveness that goes against the call of Vatican II for the church to ally with society in its effort to promote the reign of God?

4. Can their approach to catechesis, which is essentially cognitive and academic, be made compatible with the current insights of the *GDC*, which views discipleship/conversion as the proper goal?

5. Is their current support based on parents' desires to protect their children from what they consider the dangers and deficiencies of public education? Are they therefore in danger of becoming (or at least being perceived) as private schools serving wealthier Catholics?

6. Are the financial sacrifices parishes are required to make to maintain them justified in terms of the proportionate number of children served? In terms of their effectiveness in handing down the faith? How can we accurately measure this effectiveness?

7. Is the proportion of the budget committed to maintaining them equitable? Or, considering the proportionally small number served, is the commitment to maintain schools

unfairly preventing parishes from providing the funds needed for other essential ministries?

8. What responsibility does the church have to help society maintain and improve public schools, especially those that serve the poor in the inner cities? How should such responsibility affect church advocacy for school choice and for vouchers?

9. While granting their qualifications in academic subjects, are the majority of Catholic school teachers, especially the younger ones, sufficiently grounded in the faith to be committed and competent catechists?

We do not propose to attempt to address all the issues raised here. Our concern is basically with discerning the proper role of the schools in our overall catechetical ministry, especially in the light the *GDC* now sheds on the nature and purpose of that ministry. Provided the church can satisfactorily address the above issues, we are confident our schools can continue to be very effective as instruments for catechesis. What follows is an attempt to suggest some directions for our schools to pursue in their commitment to fulfill their catechetical role at the beginning of the third millennium. It is safe to presume that much of what we say is already well known to our school leaders.

## QUALITY OF STAFF

The most critical task our schools face revolves around the recruitment and formation of staff. Even more important than academic knowledge of the faith is the commitment of the administration and faculty to their own growth in discipleship. We cannot expect them to be able to give the essential witness to discipleship required of catechists today if they lack this commitment in their own lives.

Experience shows that to a large extent the success of our schools in handing on the faith in the past can be traced to the witness of faith provided by the religious who staffed them. Though some of the content and methods now seem quaint, the fact remains that these religious possessed a transparent love for the church and were totally dedicated to living out the message of the gospel as they understood it at the time. It was this witness, which transcended their lessons and methods, that was ultimately responsible for their success in generating a similar love for the church and dedication to gospel values in those they taught.

It is not a question of whether or not laity can provide a comparable witness of discipleship. As the priestly people their baptism ordained them to be, they certainly can be effective witnesses. In fact, this witness can be even more valuable than that formerly provided by religious. It can serve to demonstrate to today's children and youth that everyone, not just clergy and religious, are called to discipleship. But for this to happen, it is essential that the school administrators (principals, boards, pastors) call for this commitment to discipleship in their faculties and provide them with the guidance, support, and formation required to foster their growth as disciples. It is primarily this personal commitment to discipleship among administration and faculty that is required if our schools are to obtain the Catholic identity they now so avidly seek. It is this kind of commitment that can ensure that our schools will continue to be effective agents for catechesis in the third millennium. If they fail to acquire this kind of commitment among administration and staff, it is doubtful that they would deserve continued financial support, especially when that means limiting funds for other essential ministries.

## CATECHESIS IN AN ACADEMIC SETTING

In stressing that we need to free catechesis from the academic model, it may seem that we are implying that catechesis should never be provided in an academic setting. This is not the case. The basic problem with the academic model is that it arose in response to and continues to foster the notion that faith is essentially cognitive. We are striving to reaffirm that faith is essentially relational in nature and that our catechesis should be designed primarily to foster a relationship with Jesus. This is not to say there is no cognitive dimension to faith or that catechesis provided in an academic setting has no value. While maintaining its academic setting for catechesis our schools, together with all those in catechetical ministry, will need to make some adaptations in keeping with the direction provided by the *GDC*. For example, they will need to reshape their message in keeping with the principles of inculturation. They will often need to employ the principles of new evangelization. They will have to take into consideration the signs of the times in developing their programs. They will have to include the principles of praxis in their methodology to the degree the academic model allows it.

Thus, in the essentially academic setting of the school to employ the academic model is quite appropriate—provided certain adaptations are made. Perhaps more important, our schools will need to make greater efforts to balance their classroom catechesis with opportunities for encounter and with experiences designed to foster the essentially relational nature of discipleship. Fortunately, the need for greater balance is now becoming widely recognized, accepted, and addressed.

In their efforts to reclaim and/or maintain their Catholic identity, many Catholic schools have indeed become aware that it is not enough to provide religion classes. They now recognize the need to provide the overall ambiance of a faith community and to complement their academic program with opportunities for encounter and with opportunities to put faith in practice: liturgical and retreat experiences; service projects aimed at fostering awareness and concern for the needs of the poor and marginalized; policies and programs designed to promote the gospel values of inclusivity, tolerance, mutual respect, cooperation, and caring.

Such schools, when staffed by faculty personally committed to growth in discipleship, will continue to be effective catechetical agents well positioned to implement the insights of the *GDC* and to carry forth the catechetical agenda in the third millennium. Achieving and maintaining this kind of balance is not always easy. A very real tension exists between this commitment to being a school of discipleship and the ongoing challenge to provide a quality education in secular subjects.

Unfortunately, there are some schools that have become so preoccupied with maintaining or achieving academic excellence in secular subjects that they continue to consider it enough to provide religion classes with an occasional devotional or other religious activity. It seems some of our Catholic high schools, designed primarily as college prep schools, are especially prone to this. Some parochial schools in more affluent suburban areas also feel pressure to focus more on academic excellence than on fostering growth in discipleship. Much of this pressure comes from the parents whose support is essential if the schools are to survive. We address this issue next.

## PARENTS, CATHOLIC SCHOOLS, AND CATECHESIS

Parents instinctively want the best for their children and just as instinctively seek to protect them from harm. It is no surprise, therefore, that conscientious parents seek quality academic education in a safe, caring environment. If we are honest, we must admit that this basic parental instinct, more than concern for faith, is often the motive for parents to enroll their children in Catholic schools. Some parents have become convinced that Catholic schools are better equipped to provide a quality education and safe environment than their local public schools.

Even when faith or religious education is the primary concern, too often parents view this aspect of the school's function primarily in terms of fostering basic religious practices, moral principles, and self-discipline in the child. They do not demand or expect the school to foster discipleship per se. They cannot be faulted, because no one has told them—and they remain unaware—that the true nature of faith consists in growth in such discipleship. Continuing to operate out the understanding that faith is essentially cognitive, they are content in knowing that religion is being taught and that their child is receiving satisfactory grades in that subject. And they understandably presume that they can fulfill their own obligation to nurture faith in their children by delegating that task to the school.

199

Unfortunately, studies indicate that a significant number of parents who send their children to Catholic schools today do not have even the admirable if flawed religious motivations just described. They tend to be more concerned with the number of computers the school has than with its choice of religion texts. They tend to be more concerned with the qualifications of the math and science teachers than with the qualifications of those teaching religion. Precisely because they are enthusiastic and often generous supporters of their children's school—albeit for the wrong motives—they either directly or indirectly exert considerable pressure on the administration to give more attention to maintaining academic excellence than to the school's catechetical ministry. Such parents might well have no problem with reducing the number or length of the religion classes if that would allow more time for adding a foreign language or a computer lab to the curriculum, for example.

If Catholic schools are to remain viable catechetical agents in the third millennium, it will be necessary for them to do two things. First, as is the case with all of us involved in catechetical ministry, the school's leaders will need to help their well-intentioned parents to recognize that faith essentially involves discipleship and not just knowledge of religious truths. They will need to help parents recognize their own call to discipleship, their need to respond to that invitation, and their need to provide a witness of discipleship to their children. Parent must be helped to realize that without the support of their own commitment to discipleship, the school is extremely limited in its ability to nurture faith in their children.

Second, school officials must have the courage to resist the pressure of those well-meaning but misguided parents whose primarily motivation for choosing a Catholic school is its ability to provide a quality academic education in a disciplined setting. School administrators must not allow such parents—who are often as energetic in voicing their views as they are generous in offering their financial support—to distract them from the real purpose and mission of the Catholic school. School leaders must remain convinced that it is better to maintain a small, financially struggling but authentically Catholic school than to operate a large, academically successful and financially secure academic institution that has lost its soul.

None of what we are saying will be easy to achieve. But because the current challenge to "educate" the adult community regarding the true nature of faith and their call to discipleship is a task shared by all those involved in catechetical ministry, school leaders can expect to find the allies in their effort.

## SCHOOLS, EVANGELIZATION, AND SOCIAL JUSTICE

Both in this country and in Europe much of the Catholic school ministry was initially directed primarily toward the poor. In Europe, where the availability of universal public education is relatively new, it was often only the children of the wealthy who had access to education. In response to this inequity any number of religious communities arose during the seventeenth through nineteenth centuries committed to providing education to the poor and marginalized. In the United States this same kind of educational ministry was directed by these same religious communities toward the Catholic immigrant poor.

Today's Catholic-school parents are expected to pay a much greater share of the education costs through tuition and other forms of support. Though few schools by policy turn away children whose parents cannot afford the tuition, rising tuition costs are de facto moving Catholic schools in the direction of becoming more and more exclusive. Some critics now accuse the schools, perhaps unfairly, of becoming havens for the affluent, who can afford to escape what they consider the deficiencies (and dangers) of public education.

This gradual but dangerous movement toward becoming private schools is perhaps most evident in the current trend to close inner-city Catholic schools while at the same time building ever larger and better equipped Catholic schools in the suburbs. Ironically, those same suburbs also provide excellent public education in a safe environment, so children would not be deprived of a good (and safe) education if the Catholic schools were not built. The children left behind in the inner cities often have no choice but to attend substandard schools with less than ideal conditions. Fortunately, there are a number of parishes and some dioceses that continue to take responsibility for providing education for the poor. Also, a number of religious communities still involved in operating schools are now dedicating their efforts almost exclusively to providing education for the poor. But it is safe to say that most church leaders and the Catholic education community at large, though sympathetic to the ideal of serving the poor, continue to direct their energies, resources, and personnel almost exclusively toward providing education for the more affluent Catholic population.

In most cases we cannot expect the parents in the inner city to be able to support a Catholic school, though there are a number of stories of heroic efforts to keep a particular inner-city school open. If the church at large is to follow its own teachings about social justice, it needs to reexamine its responsibility to maintain inner-city schools out of concern for the poor. This reevaluation is critical if our commitment to Catholic education in third millennium is to be justified—and just.

It must be added that where inner-city schools are being maintained by the church, they are proving to be excellent vehicles for evangelization, not so much through direct proclamation but through their witness of practical concern and commitment to the marginalized. Given the overall call for the church to reclaim evangelization as its most fundamental and essential mission, it seems imperative that the Catholic education community also give serious thought to its own potential and responsibility as an agent of evangelization, especially to the poor and marginalized.

## ARE SCHOOLS NECESSARY FOR THE CHURCH'S CATECHETICAL MINISTRY?

No one questions that when they originated in this country our Catholic schools provided an essential catechetical service and did so with great success. No one, especially those who are dedicating their lives to ministry in our Catholic schools today, will deny that our schools continue to be one of our most effective tools for catechesis. Nevertheless, we must still ask a painful and controversial question: Are Catholic schools necessary today?

We would not have to ask this question if the church had adequate funding to support the schools *and* support its other essential ministries in an equitable manner. The fact is, even with recent policies that require users (parents) to pay a greater proportion of the cost and creative efforts at fundraising, most parish schools continue to absorb a disproportionate amount of the parish budget. Other parish ministries clearly suffer as a result, including the catechetical ministry provided for those not attending the parish school—even though it may enroll a much greater number of children and youth than the school.

It must also be noted that much of the cost of operating a school has little or nothing to do with catechesis per se. It is the academic program with its requirements for faculty and modern equipment that makes operating a school such an expensive enterprise. In defense of the schools, some will be quick to point out that the school are effective catechetical agents precisely because they provide a total ambiance of faith formation and overall character development within an academic setting, not just religion classes. However, it is a proven fact that parishes without schools can provide an excellent and equally effective catechetical program for their children and youth when they have a supportive pastor and establish an adequate budget for their program. Also it is a proven fact that character formation is rooted more in the home than in any institution. Since it is possible to provide good catechetical ministry without schools today—something that may not always have been the case—is there adequate justification to maintain academic institutions which, in terms of their role as catechetical agents, are simply no longer cost efficient?

It must be clearly stated that in theory there is nothing wrong with the church operating academic institutions. Education is a basic human value and quite worthy of the church's attention. No one can argue that our schools, precisely as academic institutions, have not equipped countless Catholics to assume roles of leadership in society and in the church, and that they continue to have that potential. But our schools cannot presume that they are responsible for all the Catholic leaders that have arisen over the years. Just as many Catholic leaders have arisen without benefit of Catholic school education, including a number of our present bishops.

So our question is not intended to impugn the past success nor the continued potential of our schools both as very effective catechetical agents and as valuable academic institutions. However, if the Catholic schools, despite their proven effectiveness, are not in fact essential for carrying out the church's catechetical mission, we are not only allowed to ask but are obligated to ask if they are limiting the church's ability to provide that ministry to those not attending Catholic schools—as well as detracting from its capability to provide other and sometimes more important ministries. It is essentially a question of whether schools at this point in time should continue to be given the priority status they now enjoy when it comes to allotting the church's limited resources.

We ask this question in the context of catechesis and the schools' historic role in that ministry. The church has the duty to provide the best possible catechesis it can to as many of its people as possible. That is the given. How it chooses to do so when a variety of options are available becomes a matter of stewardship and justice. So we are suggesting that the church review its commitment to maintaining schools today in the light of its overall duty to provide catechesis. Have circumstances changed sufficiently that it is no longer necessary or financially feasible to use schools as one of its chief means for providing catechesis?

The church certainly has the right to operate academic institutions, and we have even suggested it may have the obligation in justice to provide that service to the poor in some instances. Whether the church should operate academic institutions that primarily serve the more affluent classes is another question, connected to but distinct from our catechetical question. It lies outside the scope of this book, however, and needs to be addressed as a separate issue in another forum.

Our concern remains catechetical. We can summarize as follows:

- Are today's Catholic schools an essential format for carrying out our catechetical ministry?
- If the faith community says yes, then it has the obligation to find a more equitable way to finance them so that they do not impede the church's ability to provide other equally essential ministries, including catechesis to those not attending Catholic schools.

## CONCLUSION

Because Catholic schools have become such an integral part of "who we are" as a church in the United States and because of the unquestioned good they have been able to achieve, we are no doubt going to continue to support them. From a catechetical point of view, the challenge to the schools is make the necessary adaptation called for by the *GDC* in terms of the recruitment and formation of personnel and the structuring of their catechetical content and programs to ensure that they foster discipleship. In many ways our schools are already making significant progress in those areas.

The larger questions related to how the school ministry can be supported without detriment to our other equally and sometimes more critical ministries are much more challenging. Determining the proper relationship of our schools to other issues such as our responsibility to help provide education for the poor and our call to be an evangelizing influence is equally challenging. These concerns demand the attention of the entire church, not just the catechetical community.

# 12

# Some Concluding Thoughts

By way of a brief summary we want to recall that the first premise of this work has been that the Second Vatican Council called for and initiated a renewal of catechetical ministry that is yet to be completed. A second premise has been that we can find in the recently published *General Directory for Catechesis* an outline or "agenda" for completing that renewal. We have attempted in this book to identify and then explore the implications of what we consider the most important of these agenda items presented in the *GDC*. Besides the call to redefine the goal of catechesis in terms of discipleship, some of other agenda items we identified included the need to address inculturation, evangelization, and the signs of the times as these affect how we structure our programs and articulate the content of our catechesis. The critical need for effective catechetical leadership in our time is another item.

As stated repeatedly in Part I above, the lynch pin for achieving such a renewal will be our ability to reclaim *discipleship with Jesus* as the overarching goal of our catechesis. This is what provides both the rationale and the framework for effecting the required paradigm shift in how we think about and how we do catechesis. As we tried to demonstrate, reclaiming discipleship with Jesus as the proper goal of catechesis leads immediately to the need to rethink the content of our catechesis, the way we structure our programs, and the methods we employ. The biggest challenge we face will be to "let go of" the schooling model that has served us so well for over four hundred years.

We wish to stress again that the agenda we have identified in no way exhausts the riches contained in the *GDC* either for understanding the nature of our ministry and for taking steps to renew it. We are confident, however, that if the catechetical community aggressively pursues the agenda we have identified, it will be taking major steps toward achieving the desired renewal.

Understandably, we can anticipate various criticisms to our proposals among the catechetical community. Two immediately come to mind. First, some may point out that many of the ideas here are not all that new and have been the basis for "failed" experiments at various times over the past thirty years. Others have already been successfully integrated into the mainstream of catechetical programs. Second, some of those "in the trenches" of parish ministry may complain that our proposals for restructuring parish programs are too impractical, especially given the limitations of time and personnel available today. I can agree with the first criticism insofar as many of the ideas *have* been around for some time. However, we maintained in the early chapters and repeat here that circumstances have changed radically over the past thirty years and the times are now much more propitious for successfully implementing concepts like the "relational model." Also, it remains our contention that certain ideas like shared praxis have not so much been integrated as they have been co-opted into our programs. In response to the criticism that the proposals are too impractical, we repeat that they will seem impractical only if we continue to consider knowledge and orthodoxy as the primary goals for catechesis and continue to attempt to use the schooling model as the framework for achieving those goals. However, if we truly embrace discipleship as the goal and move beyond the schooling model, to the relational model the proposals here, though still challenging, can be implemented with proper adaptation in virtually any situation.

It is important to recall here that "proper adaptation" is another critical premise underlying the proposals made in this book. As frequently stated, we have not attempted to present a detailed "how to" manual for carrying out these proposals. Circumstances vary from parish to parish within a diocese and from diocese to diocese within the country. There is no "one size fits all" formula for establishing small groups, for recruiting and training catechists to facilitate them, for inviting children to participate, for educating parents regarding proper goals of catechesis, for making the transition from "school year" to "year long" catechesis. Most important, serious study and experimentation will be required before we can hope to develop effective and comprehensive apprentice manuals for various age groups to replace current textbooks. Thus, as stated in the introduction, our hope has been to provide a catalyst for initiating this kind of discussion, experimentation, and development within the catechetical community. It was never our intention to provide it with a new program.

Finally, some closing thoughts may help to put the proposals contained in this book and the overall issue of the renewal of catechesis into proper perspective. A kind of symbiotic connection exists between ecclesiology (the church's self-understanding) and catechesis. One's ecclesiology tends to define and shape both the goal and the appropriate methodology for catechesis. One's catechesis, in turn, tends to defend and foster the ecclesiology that generated it. So catechetical renewal never takes place in a vacuum. An authentic renewal in catechesis presumes that a shift is taking place from one form of ecclesiology to another. Thus, the renewal of catechesis initiated after the Council of Trent can be traced to a shift in the ecclesiology that same council promoted. Likewise, the renewal of catechesis initiated by the Second Vatican Council reflects a shift in ecclesiology espoused by that council. Just as the shift in ecclesiology initiated by Vatican II is not yet completed, so the catechetical renewal it fostered is not yet completed.

Even the casual observer of the church's life will note that there has been a growing resistance to the shift in the church's self-understanding begun at Vatican II. In some instances there have been attempts to reverse various teachings of Vatican II. A number of small but well-organized and quite vocal conservative (and sometimes reactionary) lay groups have allied with a number of well-placed, conservative, and equally vocal members of the hierarchy to foster this resistance. No one can deny the effectiveness of their efforts in any number of cases to impede the implementation of Vatican II. It is not surprising, therefore, that efforts to renew catechesis along the lines suggested by Vatican II have met with similar resistance and continue to do so.

The agenda for catechetical renewal we have presented here is rooted in and reflects the shift in ecclesiology fostered by Vatican II. Thus, any hope for the successful implementation of our suggestions for renewing catechesis presupposes that the ecclesiology of Vatican II becomes the self-understanding of the majority of Catholics, despite the resistance by the more conservative minority. It is our personal conviction that such a shift in the church's self-understanding will in fact be completed within the first half of the twenty-first century. Seeds planted by Vatican II have taken deep root and are beginning to bear fruit. Certain sociological, economic, and political developments in the past fifty years have made the ecclesiology that existed prior to Vatican II untenable, even though desperate efforts continue to be made by certain church leaders to preserve that ecclesiology. Various crises and movements within the church that have been precipitated by those sociological, economic, and political developments are making it imperative that the church rethink its nature and mission. The priest shortage, for example, requires us to reexamine the nature and role of the ordained priesthood as well as the nature and role of the priesthood of all the baptized. It also requires that we find new ways to organize ourselves at the parish and diocesan levels. The continuing challenges made by women to the appropriateness of the patriarchal model whether in government, business, or religion are another example. They call the church to reexamine the role women should play in its ministry and governance. Also, now that political and economic dominance by Western countries can no longer be presumed as normative or even desirable, the Roman Church, with its roots and base in that same Western society, is finding it necessary to rethink its proper role and relationship to Catholic churches in the rest of the world and to other world religions as well.

We mention these more salient and obvious challenges the church is facing simply to make the point that, as much as some may wish it possible, the church cannot return to the life and self-understanding it had prior to Vatican II. A renewed ecclesiology is definitely emerging. The Spirit will not be denied.

We ask that you view the proposals for the renewal of catechesis made in the book within the context of this emerging ecclesiology. It is in this way that both their validity and timeliness can best be judged.

# Appendix 1

# The Catechism
# of the Catholic Church

It may seem strange that the *Catechism of the Catholic Church*, a document so integral to catechetical ministry, has been relegated to an appendix in a book purporting to offer direction for the renewal of catechesis in the third millennium. This decision does not reflect an attitude that the *CCC* is unimportant or does not have a critical role to play in our ministry. Rather, it is dictated by the nature and purpose of the document as described by its authors in the material accompanying its promulgation.

The *CCC* is by nature an authoritative compendium of the truths of our faith. As such, it is intended to be a reference and resource for developing catechetical materials and programs. It is not, nor is it designed to be, a textbook or a program. As the introductory material makes quite clear, it does not attempt, for example, to present material in light of the various stages of cognitive development or readiness. It espouses no particular methodology. Being intended for use by the universal church, it seeks to transcend any particular cultural or ethnic bias. Thus, as the introductory material also stresses, the *CCC* by its very nature requires adaptation before its value in catechetical ministry can be actualized. It calls for and presumes the development of national and regional catechisms (which have been slow in coming, we might add) that inculturate its content and make it more understandable and acceptable to various cultures and ethnic groups. It calls for and presumes the authors of catechetical material designed for

211

specific age groups and cultures will make similar adaptations in language and metaphors to make its truth accessible to their intended audiences. In short, the CCC by nature is intended to remain in the background of our ministry, a resource to be referred to when developing our materials and programs. As such, it is an invaluable, authoritative, and unifying resource that is worthy of respect.

Even when used as such a resource, the CCC is not intended to be the only resource we are to use. It is not the first such authoritative compendium the church has developed. It therefore needs to take its place beside any number of other documents that provide us authoritative insights into our faith, a prime example being the documents of the Second Vatican Council, the riches of which we are just now coming to appreciate. Nor is the CCC's particular articulation of our faith, authoritative as it is, the last word. As the CCC itself states, our understanding of revelation continues to evolve and remains open to new articulations and new emphases. A simple comparison between the catechism of the Council of Trent and the CCC will bear witness to that fact.

In this context it is important to note that competent scholars and theologians point to certain deficiencies and shortcomings in the CCC's treatment of some topics and/or in the undue emphasis it places on others. Most notably, perhaps, its use of scripture does not always reflect current scripture scholarship and advances in exegesis. But there is no need here to give a detailed review of such critiques. These are readily available elsewhere. We only wish to stress that, as good as it is, when used as a catechetical resource the CCC needs to be balanced by and complemented with other equally valuable resources.

On the positive side, in format, style, and organization it is innovative and refreshing compared to previous catechisms and similar compendiums. It maintains a positive tone. It effectively uses quotations from various heroes of our tradition to give it a more human face. Its summaries are for the most part helpful, though they can sometimes be misleading. Its cross-reference system makes it very "user friendly" as a resource and also serves to demonstrate the unity and close interrelationship that exists among the various truths of our faith.

There is one tragic flaw in the English translation available to us of the CCC, however, which should not go unmentioned. It is rooted in the decision to reject the original English translation, which was excellent in style and was very careful to avoid the use of exclusive language. Unfortunately, the official translation that was finally approved is thoroughly sexist in language. Though accuracy requires that sexist language found in various quotations from documents in previous ages be maintained, there is no excuse for the sexist language found in the narrative portions of the text. This flaw makes what is in so many other ways an excellent resource potentially and unnecessarily offensive to half of the church—and to an even greater proportion of catechists, since the majority of them are women. Finally, it should be noted that this flaw cannot be attributed to its original authors and fortunately does not affect the accuracy and validity of its content.

Having said all this, we need to ask what role the CCC has in our catechetical agenda for the third millennium. Stated simply, we are to use it as it is by its nature intended to be used, as a valuable resource in the development of catechetical materials and programs. It definitely deserves a respected place in our library, alongside the other equally valuable doctrinal resources and reference books available to us. We also should consider it part of our agenda to advocate for and participate in the development of national and, perhaps more important, regional catechisms that adapt and inculturate its content, making its riches more useful and available for our ministry. Its true potential as a resource for our ministry in the future will be realized only when such adaptations are produced.

At the same time we need to be aware that, though not in any way inherently harmful, the CCC has the potential to be a serious obstacle to our efforts to renew catechesis along the lines intended by Vatican II. It should be noted that the council, in its effort to move away from an over-emphasis on the cognitive dimension of faith, voted not to issue a catechism, though the Council of Trent had set such a precedent. It regarded its documents themselves sufficient to develop a general directory for catechesis to guide us in our efforts to foster faith in the coming generations.

The decision to publish a catechism reflects, and at least in part was motivated by, the desire to refocus our attention on the more cognitive dimension of our faith. That there is a cognitive dimension to our faith is, of course, a given. But this focus on the cognitive dimension of faith inherent by nature in catechisms, when viewed in the context of the worldwide publicity and importance that accompanied the CCC's publication in 1994, can tend quite naturally to have the effect of reemphasizing "education for membership" and de-emphasizing discipleship as the proper goal of catechesis.

Thus, we have no argument with the document or its content per se. But we need to point out that its very existence and what it implies about the nature of faith can become an obstacle in our efforts to renew catechesis. It can provide those opposed to that renewal with an authoritative argument and a tool for reverting to the goals and methods of catechesis that existed prior to Vatican II. Even a casual observation of the "catechetical scene" today will illustrate that such a movement exists, bolstered and energized in no small part by the existence of the CCC.

In summary, the decision to treat the CCC as an appendix in our catechetical agenda for the third millennium is something of a symbolic attempt to indicate its proper role in that agenda. It certainly has an important role, but that role calls for it to remain in the background as a foundational document and invaluable resource. We would be misusing it and actually hindering our efforts to renew catechesis (and the church) if we allowed it be used in any other way.

# Appendix 2

# Confirmation and the Catechetical Agenda

The controversy that continues to swirl around the issues of the proper age and order for celebrating the sacrament of confirmation is somewhat symptomatic of the overall lack of unity and focus that has befallen the catechetical ministry in recent years. We wish to address those issues related to confirmation briefly here in the hope that we can illustrate how the paradigm shift we have proposed in this book can serve not only to resolve the controversy over the sacrament of confirmation but also restore a sense of unity and focus to our entire ministry.

First some background, which will no doubt be quite familiar to veteran catechists. Liturgists together with theologians have effectively demonstrated that confirmation is to be understood and celebrated as a sacrament of initiation, intimately tied to baptism and first Eucharist. This theology, in turn, supports the liturgists' position that the proper order of celebration is baptism, confirmation and first Eucharist. This ordering of the sacraments presents no problem, of course, when dealing with adult converts who proceed through the RCIA process. It becomes more problematic when we are dealing with the question of when to confirm children baptized as infants. Some liturgists have advocated that we confirm infants immediately after baptism in a single ritual. Others have challenged the present practice of infant baptism and have advocated that we delay the celebration of both sacraments until the children are older and can be enrolled in a catechumenate. For a variety of reasons neither of these two proposals has received any real support from the hierarchy, the people in general, or the catechetical community in particular.

Nevertheless, some dioceses and their catechetical leaders, convinced of the validity of the liturgists' position and wishing to restore the proper order as identified by them, are choosing to confirm children at a very early age, around seven or eight, so the sacrament can be celebrated prior to first Eucharist. Because of the young age of the confirmands, this practice has the obvious drawback of allowing time for only the most minimal and rudimentary catechetical preparation. The majority of dioceses and their catechetical leaders, even though they might agree in theory with the liturgists' position, have shown that they are unwilling to forego what they consider adequate catechetical preparation simply for the sake of maintaining the proper liturgical order of celebration. So they delay the celebration of confirmation of those baptized as infants until some time after they have received first Eucharist. But there is no unanimity on how long that delay should be. A significant number continue or have returned to the practice of confirming at the more traditional age of twelve to fourteen. Some opt for a slightly earlier age and confirm during the middle school years. About half of the dioceses have adopted the practice of confirming somewhere in the later teens, and a few dioceses have set no policy, leaving the decision to the local parishes. It is worth noting that the theological and/or pastoral rationales given for confirming at each of these different ages are as varied as the ages themselves.

Now let us briefly review the theology of the sacrament itself apart from liturgical considerations regarding the proper order for its celebration. Here too veteran catechists will find themselves in familiar territory. Confirmation's origin, nature, and purpose have their roots, of course, in the Pentecost experience recorded in Acts 2. There is no agreement among scholars on when and how the first disciples were "baptized," but it is safe to assume they had a baptismal experience prior to Pentecost. From the account of the Pentecost experience given in Acts, as well as from the events that

216

immediately preceded and followed it, this much is irrefutably clear. This first Pentecost experience marked the end of the preparation or apprenticeship of these disciples of Jesus. The outpouring of the Spirit it signified had the effect of fully empowering and commissioning them to go forth and boldly to continue Jesus' mission of proclaiming the reign of God. We do not wish to make too much of it, but in terms of the liturgists' present concern for the proper ordering of the sacraments, it is interesting to note that these first disciples received their first Eucharist prior to and not after their confirmation.

Regardless of when it is celebrated, therefore, the theological nature and purpose of confirmation are intended to mark the end of the disciples' initial formation and preparation for ministry (apprenticeship) by fully and officially empowering and commissioning them to assume their role and responsibility for carrying out the church's mission. As a sacrament of initiation, therefore, it is designed to initiate them not so much into the church, which was already achieved at baptism, but into the mission of that church.

Let us assume that we do begin to understand the goal of catechesis in terms of discipleship formation. Let us further assume that we begin to approach and structure the catechesis provided for children and youth baptized in infancy as a kind of apprentice program for discipleship similar to the one provided the very first disciples by Jesus prior to their Pentecost experience. It seems we can then make a very strong case, based on quite solid sacramental theology as well as on sound pastoral practice, for proposing that confirmation be viewed as the sacramental celebration that marks the end of that apprenticeship and the beginning (initiation) of the disciples' official mission and ministry within the community of disciples. Understood in this way there is no inherent reason why confirmation needs to be celebrated prior to first Eucharist. Considered as one of the three sacraments of initiation, first Eucharist primarily marks the child's being invited for the first time to take his or her rightful place at the eucharistic table, a right that was received at baptism. There is no reason the child should not be regularly nourished at that table as an integral part of his or her apprenticeship, an apprenticeship designed to culminate in confirmation.

Though liturgists may point to the long tradition supporting the reception of confirmation prior to first Eucharist, that tradition arose within the context of a catechumenate intended primarily for adult converts, a catechumenate designed as the very kind of apprenticeship we are advocating. Ritually joining one's official initiation into the community (baptism) and initiation into mission (confirmation) and culminating that ritual with the celebration of first Eucharist made preeminent sense in that context, just as it does for adults converts being apprenticed for discipleship through the RCIA process today. However, demanding that we restore this ritual unity even though circumstances have been radically changed by the practice of infant baptism and even though it requires that we confirm children at a very young age seems rather legalistic.

Some liturgists and the catechists are quick to stress the power of the sacraments to effect what they signify as justification for continuing to confirm young children. In this context they often point to the practice of the Eastern Church to confirm and communicate infants at their baptism. This *ex opere operato* view of the sacraments, though valid, focuses more on assuring us that the sacraments are efficacious regardless of the "worthiness" of the one administering them. Thus we are assured by this doctrine that we still have access to the grace and power of the sacraments even when we do not have access to "good" sacramental ministers. But sacramental theology just as strongly emphasizes that the efficacy of the sacraments requires the proper disposition in those receiving them. The sacraments are not magic. Our present understanding of and belief in their nature and purpose, our attentiveness during their celebration, our conscious intentions for approaching them all have some effect on what "actually happens" to us when we receive them. It is certainly not accurate to say nothing happens when we confirm very young children. But just as in the baptism of infants, what is signified by the sacrament of confirmation does not automatically become actualized in the child without ongoing nurture and catechesis after the fact. We can defend the tradition of infant baptism on various grounds, both theological and pastoral, especially since the church's ritual makes it quite clear that it presumes that parents will assume their responsibility to provide the necessary formal catechesis (or apprenticeship) as the child comes of age. It seems harder to defend early confirmation simply to preserve a ritual unity, especially because the sacrament is intended by its nature to mark the end and not the beginning of apprenticeship as a disciple and by nature does not carry with it a parental obligation to provide further catechesis.

So, when is the proper age for celebrating confirmation? Chronologically speaking, there is no proper age. From our perspective, confirmation is properly celebrated when the person has been adequately apprenticed as a disciple and thus possesses the maturity of faith and age required to be able to understand and fully participate in the church's mission. In that light it is doubtful that the sacrament is appropriate for very young children. In fact, it can be argued that in our society today such an apprenticeship needs to extend through childhood and youth—and for some perhaps even into young adulthood. At the same time there are individuals who tend to mature quite rapidly as disciples and may be ready at an earlier age. Such is the nature of a true apprenticeship. Though chronological age plays a role, in a true apprentice program people grow at their own pace and not according to grades in school. In such a program individuals are invited, or will come forth to request confirmation when they feel they are sufficiently grounded in discipleship to be ready for this next step. A true apprentice program, like its counterpart, the RCIA, should be a somewhat open-ended process.

We hope the above analysis illustrates two points. First, from a catechetical perspective there is no compelling theological or pastoral reason for altering our programs artificially in an attempt to preserve ritual unity and the proper order for the reception of the sacraments of initiation as advocated by our liturgists. Second, if the catechetical community adopts as its proper goal discipleship formation provided through a discipleship apprentice program, there is no further need to argue about the proper age for confirmation. The proper time for confirmation is whenever the person has been adequately apprenticed as a disciple and possesses the maturity of faith and age required to be able to understand and fully to participate in the church's mission. Thus we can once again attain theological unity as a catechetical community in our approach to confirmation. We can also agree on the proper time for celebrating the sacrament without demanding that every diocese or parish conform to some artificial and arbitrary chronological age.

# Notes

1. Thomas H. Groome, *Christian Religious Education—Sharing Our Story and Vision* (San Francisco, Calif: Harper & Row, 1980).
2. For a complete treatment of these five movements, refer to ibid., Part II, esp. chaps. 9 and 10.
3. Rembert Weakland, "Reflections for Rome," *America* 178, no. 13 (April 18, 1998).

# Bibliography

## CHURCH DOCUMENTS

*Catechesi Tradendae.* Washington, D.C.: United States Catholic Conference, 1979.

*The Catechism of the Catholic Church.* Washington, D.C.: United States Catholic Conference, 1994.

*The Documents of Vatican II.* Edited by Walter M. Abbott, S.J. New York: Guild Press, 1966.

*The General Catechetical Directory.* Washington, D.C.: United States Catholic Conference, 1971.

*The General Directory for Catechesis,* Washington, D.C.: United States Catholic Conference, 1997.

## GENERAL WORKS

Babin, Pierre, with Iannone Mercedes. *The New Era in Religious Communication,* Minneapolis, Minn.: Fortress Press, 1992.

Bishops' Committee for Catechesis and Adult Christian Education, Bishops' Conference of England and Wales. *A Gift Destined to Grow—An Invitation to Study the General Directory for Catechesis.* Chelmsford, England: Rejoice Publications, 1999.

Groome, Thomas H. *Christian Religious Education—Sharing Our Story and Vision.* San Francisco, Calif.: Harper & Row, 1980.

222

Kelly, Liam. *Catechesis Revisited—Handing on the Faith Today,* Mahwah, N.J.: Paulist Press, 2000.

Marthaler, Berard L., ed. *Introducing the Catechism of the Catholic Church.* London: SPCK, 1994.

Rappaport, Roy A. *Ritual and Religion in the Making of Humanity.* Cambridge, England: Cambridge University Press, 1999.

Warren, Michael. *Source Book for Modern Catechetics.* 2 vol. Winona, Minn.: St. Mary's Press, 1983 (vol. 1) and 1997 (vol. 2).